ON THE ROAD city
Florence

ON THE ROAD
Editor of collection
Laura Andreini

editorial project
Forma Edizioni srl, Firenze, Italia
redazione@formaedizioni.it
www.formaedizioni.it

editorial production
Archea Associati

editorial direction
Laura Andreini

author
Laura Andreini

editorial staff
Sara Benzi
Elena Ronchi
Valentina Muscedra
Maria Giulia Caliri

graphic design
Elisa Balducci
Alberto Bolzonetti
Vitoria Muzi
Isabella Peruzzi
Mauro Sampaolesi

translations
Katy Hannan

photolithography
LAB di Gallotti Giuseppe Fulvio,
Firenze, Italia

printing
Gutenberg Press Limited,
Gudja Road, Tarxien, Malta PLA 19

First Edition: November 2017

ISBN 978-88-96780-91-6

Table of contents

Guidebook as tool

On the Road is a new collection of contemporary architecture guidebooks whose purpose is to tell about a place, whether a city or larger area, through its architectural works chosen to be visited and experienced directly.

The guidebook has a convenient special jacket that opens into a map marking the location of the architectural works and interesting sites to visit. On the back are miniature images and addresses of the architectural works described in detail within.

The book starts with short essays explaining the city or area's present day and history and outlining possible future scenarios with planned or imminent projects. Each work features of a photograph of the whole, an architectural drawing (plan or section), a short description, and facts including architect, type, year of construction, address, website, and how to visit it.

The finest architecture of each city and suggested routes are represented by this collection of not-to-be-missed, "timeless" buildings that uniquely define their settings. General information and useful tips for travelers help them optimize their visits and quickly understand the essence of the place described.

Museums, theatres, restaurants, hotels and a list of top architectural firms working in the city let visitors turn a regular trip into an opportunity for study or work.

Note: The pin pointers outside the maps at the beginning of the itineraries are viewable on the rear of the book jacket.

Florence

Laura Andreini

A guide to contemporary architecture in a city such as Florence might seem an oxymoron to certain readers. This book, part of the On the Road series, is aimed at showing how one of the Italian cities most strongly linked with its past, in fact the quintessential symbol of the Renaissance period, conceals a myriad of innovative architecture.

Florence is not a static city. It has often been guilty of long delays and a certain lack of courage in assimilating new approaches, but its way of introducing contemporary architecture into a consolidated context, is unique.

Changes with great impact began in Florence at the end of the 19th century with the urban planning transformations designed by Giuseppe Poggi, and the brief but intense period when Florence was the country's capital city. The strongly defined limits of the historic centre became blurred with the demolition of the fortifications and the city was opened up to permit expansion. In the 1930s, the Rationalist design of the Santa Maria Novella Station introduced a new form of architectural expression into the historic centre and outskirts of the city. This is the building that begins the itinerary proposed in this guide; a chronological, but also a physical beginning: a starting point for visitors to begin their architectural tour. Furthermore, it is because of the station that we are able to observe the complexity of the city. Suffice to say that in 1935, in a single day, King Vittorio Emanuele II inaugurated two buildings with completely contrasting design styles: the Station and the Central National Library (which is also included in the guide for this reason). Still today, the city has difficulty in adopting a single approach or process, this aspect contributes towards creating an interesting diversity, but also a certain degree of confusion. And the limits of the city are still expanding today. Florence is beginning to acknowledge its metropolitan nature through urban expansion and, above all, infrastructures such as tram transport that change the perception of distance. For this reason, quality contemporary architecture has moved on towards the outskirts of the city.

The guide is composed of 84 projects divided into 3 itineraries. In each itinerary, especially the tour in the historic centre, the guide includes descriptions of the most famous historic buildings of major interest. These descriptions do not profess to provide detailed information on these famous monuments, but it was impossible not to include them in the guide. They are among the main points of reference in the city and for any visitors to Florence. After all, Florence is the symbol of the Renaissance period, and in a large number of contemporary buildings, the modern composition and style always reflects strong aspects of the city's history. Perhaps this is one of the reasons that makes Florence a city that deserves its place in a guide dedicated to contemporary architecture.

Political / geographical facts

country
Italy

language
italian

area code
+39 055

coordinates
43° 46' 45'' N
11° 14' 46'' E

area
102,32 km²

population
382.808

density
3.736,77 ab./km²

time zone
UTC+1

city website
www.comune.fi.it

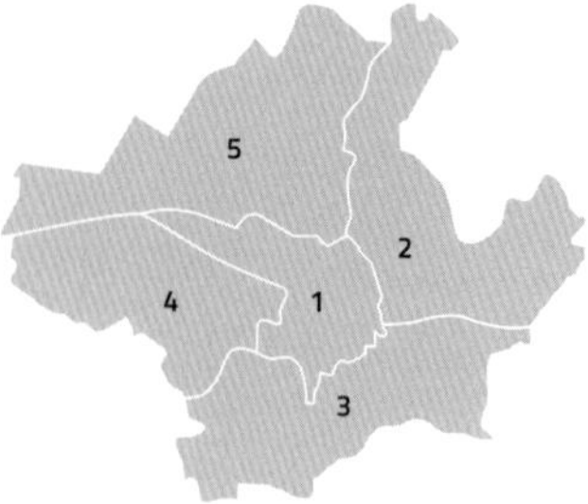

Administrative districts

1. Historic Centre
2. Campo di Marte
3. Gavinana Galluzzo
4. Isolotto Legnaia
5. Rifredi

General information
useful addresses and numbers

INFORMATION OFFICES

www.firenzeturismo.it

Infopoint Stazione
Piazza della Stazione 4
+39 055 212245
Mon - Sat / 9 am - 7 pm
Sun and holidays / 9 am - 2 pm

Tourist Information Office
Via Camillo Cavour 1r
+39 055 290832-3
Mon - Fri / 9 am - 1 pm

Infopoint Bigallo
Piazza San Giovanni 1
+39 055 288496
Mon - Sat / 9 am - 7 pm
Sun and holidays / 9 am - 2 pm

Airport Infopoint
Via del Termine 11
+39 055 315874
Mon - Sun / 9 am - 7 pm

Parco delle Cascine Visitors' Info Centre
Piazzale delle Cascine
+39 055 365707
Fri - Sun / 9 am - 7 pm

EMERGENCY SERVICES

Carabinieri 112
Police 113
Emergency medical service 118
Fire Department 115
24-hour Pharmacy 800 420707
Misericordia di Firenze
(medical treatment services) 055 212222
www.misericordia.firenze.it

URBAN TRANSPORT

Bus and Tram*
Tickets: can be bought at Ataf Points, CRAL Ataf, news stands, authorised cigarette stores and cafés, automatic vending machines, SMS text service at 4880105 (text "ATAF"); www.ataf.net

Taxi
+39 055 4242; SMS +39 334 6622550;
+29 0554300

Car sharing

Share'ngo
www.sharengo.it
+39 0586 1975772

Car2go
www.car2go.com/IT/it/florence
+39 055 4282107

Enjoy
www.enjoy.eni.com/it/firenze/home
+39 06 59881

Bicycle rentals

Mobike
mobike.com/it

Ulisse cooperativa sociale
www.bicifirenze.it

Florence By Bike
www.florencebybike.it

GENERAL CONSULATE OF THE UNITED STATES
Lungarno Amerigo Vespucci 38, 50123 Florence
Tel +39 055 266951

GENERAL CONSULATE OF FRANCE
Piazza Ognissanti 2, 50123 Florence
Tel +39 055 2302556

EMBASSY OF THE PEOPLE'S REPUBLIC OF CHINA
Via dei della Robbia 89, 50132 Florence
Tel +39 055 573889

HOW TO PHONE

From a local landline: dial local code number followed by phone number (055)

From a foreign landline: dial international code (+39) city code (055) and phone number

* Ticket categories:
Single ride (valid 90 mins), 2 or 4 rides; daily pass (1, 3 or 7 days); multi-day pass (for groups: min. 10 passengers); daily family, AGILE card, night timetable (8 pm- 3 am), volainbus (SMN Station - Vespucci Airport).

Useful tips

1. Because of its scenographic position surrounded by enchanting hill country, Florence offers countless breath-taking views. The closest panoramic view is from Piazzale Michelangelo with the nearby **Abbey of San Miniato al Monte/80** and the charming Iris Garden, open from the end of April till the end of May, easily reached on foot along the Piazza Poggi ramp; another famous landmark is the Belvedere Fortress, a pleasant walk from Costa San Giorgio. Wonderful views can be had from the hills of Fiesole and Settignano. A visit worth making in Fiesole is the Fondazione Michelucci, former home and studio of the architect whose garden provides an unexpected view of Florence. A climb to the top of the Dome of Santa Maria del Fiore or the Giotto Bell Tower gives visitors an impressive 360° view of the whole city. For a view of Florence from a different perspective, take a tour along the Arno punted in small river boats.

2. We advise those who want to visit the museums of Florence to buy a **Firenzecard**, the official Florentine museum pass. The card is valid for 72 hours after its initial use, and permits a single visit to each of the Museums on the Circuit. It grants access to permanent collections and temporary exhibitions, with priority access entry and without prior booking. For further information, check the website: www.firenzecard.it.

3. To enjoy your visit to Florence without wasting precious time, visitors can have a quick but delicious meal with the famous Florentine lampredotto tripe sandwich and a glass of wine from one of the **Lampredotto stands** dotted around the city. There are also dozens of ***vinaini***: small shops that sell casked wine by the bottle, or by the glass, often accompanied by cocktail snacks eaten at the counter. If you eat in a trattoria, be prepared to share your table with other guests, a pleasant way to meet new people. On the other hand, if you want to try the famous Florentine T-bone steak, you are in the right city! The **Mercato Centrale Firenze/14**, in the San Lorenzo quarter, also provides a chance to try a large number of local street foods, sitting at tables among the stalls of this unique street market.

4. As far as shopping is concerned, Florence has something for every taste and price range from the exclusive boutiques in **Via Tornabuoni** to the **San Lorenzo Market** which is open every day except Sundays and Mondays. The markets sell clothing, belts, wallets, and a large selection of traditional Florentine items in hand crafted leather and marbled paper.
A visit to the monuments and museums of Florence must include a stroll through the vibrant historic markets of the city: **the Covered Market of San Lorenzo** (the Mercato Centrale Firenze is located on the first floor), and the **Sant'Ambrogio** and **Porcellino Markets**. For antique lovers, we suggest a visit

to the markets held at Fortezza da Basso during the second weekend of every month. Another market not to be missed is the **Fierucola**, that sells traditional wine and food products from local farms and producers. It is held in Piazza SS. Annunziata on the first Sunday of the month, and in Piazza Santo Spirito on the third Sunday of each month. Information is available on their site: www.lafierucola.org. And if you happen to be strolling through the Parco delle Cascine on a Tuesday morning, it is worth stopping to see the long **Cascine market**, the biggest and cheapest open-air market in the city. Florence depends on its markets and the dozens of craftsmen's boutiques that can be found mostly on the southern bank of the Arno in the quarters of San Frediano, Santo Spirito and San Niccolò.

5. During certain periods of the year, Florence is especially rich in famous events. Fashion week **Pitti Immagine Uomo, Donna e Bambino** is mainly held at Fortezza da Basso, but it involves the whole city in the months of January and June.
For film fans, in Autumn, Florence hosts the **50 Days of International Cinema,** a project launched in 2007 to provide a single program and combined location for all the main Florentine film festivals with an international objective. For further information, check the site: www.50giornidicinema.it.
Florence is also a city rich in traditional events that date back centuries. During the week before the 24th of June, the **Feast Day of St John** and the famous firework displays, Piazza Santa Croce holds the famous historic football game, **Calcio Storico Fiorentino**, played between four of the historic quarters of the city.
An age-old tradition is held on Easter Sunday in Piazza del Duomo: the **Scoppio del Carro**, a tall wooden structure filled with fireworks, set on a 500-year-old cart, is pulled by a pair of white oxen through the streets in the historic centre, stopping between the Baptistery and the Cathedral. From the altar in the cathedral, the archbishop lights a flare in the shape of a dove, that travels along a wire through the centre nave until it hits the cart, setting off the fireworks.

A potential Florence

Gianni Biagi*

Florence is a city that pertains completely to the modern era as well as to all its contradictions. It is not a city easy to understand when one tries to grasp the link between its history and the evolution of Western philosophy. Florence is not only a city whose monuments are admired as the embodiment of the conventional stereotype of culture for mass tourism. It is also a city in which the unexpected occurs, and where innovations, seemingly impossible because they are overpowered by the weight of history, emerge and form layers of trends and schemes; this occurred with the Radical movement in the 1960s, and previously with the controversies and ideological conflict over the reconstruction of the parts of the city destroyed during the war. This is the basis from which one must start in order to read a city that relates in a single narrative the Spedale degli Innocenti and the Teatro dell'Opera, the Basilica of Santa Maria Novella and the Pier Luigi Nervi Stadium.

Works that are hundreds of years apart but symbolically linked by the leitmotif that unites the places and buildings of Florence and their capacity to break away from the dominant theme. In fact, architecture broke away and has been innovative ever since the 1930s, when contrasting concepts appeared simultaneously, with the Santa Maria Novella Station, a clear example of Italian Rationalism, and the Biblioteca Nazionale Centrale strongly inspired by the style of classical architecture, very tangibly indicating the cultural and ideological battle that divided the Regime. A city that embodied the vision of Giorgio La Pira, the "Sindaco Santo" (Saintly Mayor); a vision exemplified in the construction of the Isolotto social housing village. This plan included similar large-scale urban complexes, for more social housing schemes, like the Sorgane Quarter, whose construction launched the first controversies concerning mass construction on the hills of Florence. This debate was one of the main aspects of the city's 1962 General Town Planning Scheme, (Edoardo Detti described it in his essay "Il faticoso salvataggio di Firenze", in *Urbanistica*, no. 39), and continued to remain the dominant topic in the successive planning schemes that identified direct development criteria with the reutilization of abandoned buildings and the arrest of land take schemes.

An almost pedagogical route that has led the city of Florence to become, not only a great city of art on every tourist's wish-list, but perhaps more appropriately, a city of culture. A route that defines a city that is constantly creating a balance between conservation and innovation, and that instils this status in the completeness of the incomplete. A city that is seemingly stationary, but which has succeeded in breeding a new generation of architects whose works are widely and deservedly represented.

* Gianni Biagi, architect, full member of the Istituto Nazionale di Urbanistica, former Florence City Councillor for Town Planning and public executive, conducts his professional activity in Tuscany.

Twentieth century Architecture in Florence

Laura Andreini*

At the beginning of the twentieth century, Florence inherited a completely renewed urban, architectural and landscape configuration from the previous century. The main transformations involved areas in the city centre; the Jewish Ghetto was demolished and its closely packed and unhealthy urban fabric was replaced with the grandiose vision of the present Piazza della Repubblica. This renewal plan included the outskirts of the city, with a series of outstanding constructions designed and supervised by the engineer and architect, Giuseppe Poggi, aimed at adapting the city to its new role as capital of Italy. Poggi's vision was to transform Florence from an enclosed walled city into an open urban centre, modelled on great European capitals like Vienna and Paris, by creating wide ring roads to replace the historic city walls. The new ring road was also extended to the surrounding hills to form an original environmental and panoramic concept that concluded with the creation of the Piazzale Michelangelo. Unfortunately, it is well-known that the destiny of Florence as the country's capital lasted only five years, from 1865 till 1870. Inevitably, expectations for an increase in population diminished together with the immediate economic default by the city administration which blocked all construction activities, even though what had been built in such a short lapse of time was to leave an enduring mark on the history and current image of the city.

In the 1930s, in an attempt to gain public consensus through works that involved not only Florence but the whole country, the Fascist Regime began to construct a series of buildings and infrastructures that had a strong impact, not only on Florentine culture, but on a far wider scale, throughout the whole of Italy. There was some conflict between the new modern revolutionary design, and the restoration of the legendary classical style that recalled the splendour of the past.

The Santa Maria Novella Railway Station and the National Library, inaugurated in the same year, 1935, are the clearest examples of this historical and cultural dualism. In particular, the Central Station, the starting point for this itinerary, clearly shows the refined research, at the time in a completely Florentine style, directed at incorporating modern architecture within an existing historical context. In fact, it is one of the most representative examples of the Italian Rationalist style, but unlike other famous buildings, the station designed by the Gruppo Toscano (Berardi, Baroni, Gamberini, Guarnieri, Lusanna, Michelucci), shows the special attention paid to its context, directly and specifically linked with the apse of one of the most important monuments of Florence: the complex of Santa Maria Novella.

After the war, Florence was forced to focus on one of the most important aspects of post-war construction: the urgent need for housing, and above all, the reconstruction of the fragile areas in the city centre destroyed by German bombs which had targeted the most emblematic areas in the heart of Florence. The need for reconstruction provoked a discussion on "how to create architecture" in Florence, and, how to intervene in a contemporary manner in relation to the historical architectural heritage of the city. A cultural clash occurred between those who supported the "where it was and how it was" and those who endorsed new design and construction. This led to the faithful reconstruction of the wonderful 16th century bridge, the Ponte di Santa Trinita, by Bartolomeo Ammannati, but also included a cautiously more modern vision in the reconstruction of the buildings at each end of the Ponte Vecchio that had been spared from the bombing. This form of compromise was typical of the attitude of prominent modern Florentine architects. On one hand, they seemed rather hesitant to assume risks with contemporary design, and on the other they wished to move beyond the Rationalist period to reconnect with the roots of Tuscan architecture, consolidating the Italian tradition of creating a dialogue between past and present.

Some of the most renowned architects involved in this cultural debate, including famous figures like Giovanni Michelucci and Italo Gamberini, designed important buildings for Florence at this time. These included projects like the residential complex in Via Guicciardini (1945-1958), the headquarters of the Cassa di Risparmio in Via Bufalini (1953-1957), the Chiesa dell'Autostrada (1961-1964) by Michelucci, and the RAI headquarters (1962-1967) and State Archive Building (1971-1989) by Gamberini, which demonstrated the evolution of their architectural research over a century. The projects by these two great architects show a constant recurring theme that can be seen in the unavoidable link between tradition and innovation and the capacity to reflect the truest values of cultural identity through architecture; this is visible, for example, in the design of the social housing projects like Isolotto, in the North of Florence. The pupils who were more or less directly influenced by Michelucci and Gamberini included names such as Edoardo Detti, who was responsible for an apparently invisible but decisive work – the 1962 General Town Planning Scheme that was to save the hills of Florence from overbuilding. In (1972), he also designed the Indiano Bridge. Leonardo Savioli designed the very fine residential building in Via Piagentina (1964-1967) as well as the residential complex of the Sorgane quarter, together with another outstanding pupil, Leonardo Ricci – designer; however, the project was completed and strongly modified after the architect's death. He was also responsible for the Law Courts in Florence (1987-2012). Other works by the talented Leonardo Ricci, include the splendid houses in stone and reinforced concrete that form the Monterinaldi Complex. Among the pupils of Italo Gamberini, one of the names that stands out is that of Loris Macci who, among many other works, was responsible for restructuration of the Artemio Franchi Stadium (built in 1929 by Pier Luigi Nervi) for the 1990 World Football Championships. From a cultural viewpoint, the Seventies produced radical architecture that, despite being very important on an intellectual level, did not have a great impact in terms of constructed buildings, even though, from this group of young Utopians, emerged the figure of Adolfo Natalini who was to create a large number of buildings in Florence in the following years. These included the new Novoli university buildings (1993-2003), the extension of the Uffizi Museum (2003-2011), and the Museo dell'Opera del Duomo (2004-2015). In the Eighties, after his work on the headquarters of the Florentine daily newspaper, *La Nazione*, Pier Luigi Spadolini designed several important infrastructures like the Exhibition Pavilion of Fortezza da Basso (1974-1976) and, between this building and the Station, the complex of the Palazzo dei Congressi.

The third millennium brought new projects with the construction of the Novoli Quarter in the area previously occupied by the Fiat plant. The initial project had a strongly Avant-garde design, later replaced by a plan as interesting as it was nostalgic, created by Leon Krier and completed by Gabetti and Isola who designed the shopping mall in the same area. Works created in recent years, again in Novoli, include the residential complexes designed by Claudio Nardi, the university residences by studio C+S, and four buildings currently under construction, designed by Archea Associati. In the historic centre of the city, contemporary architecture has been used in interesting contexts like the renovation of the upper floor of the Mercato Centrale di San Lorenzo, realised by Archea Associati. It takes the form of a covered urban square set inside the beautiful complex designed by Mengoni in the 19th century. Another project is the excellent design by Ipostudio for the new Museo degli Innocenti in the Piazza Santissima Annunziata complex, by Brunelleschi.

Florence is currently a city undergoing transformation and revival: in infrastructures, with the construction of a new tram line system, and in architecture with the new Teatro del Maggio Musicale and the transformation of the areas of the original complex, plus the recovery, in the near future, of the area of the former tobacco plant, Manifattura Tabacchi, as well as other constructions in different areas of the city centre. The destiny and future of Florence will depend on these transformations. For this reason, as well as providing an opportunity to visit buildings that bear witness to the best 20th century architectural works in Florence, this compact guide represents an image of the State of the Art (in architectural terms) of a city that owes so much to its glorious and incomparable past.

* Laura Andreini is architect and associate professor at DIDA, University of Florence. Co-founder of Studio Archea where she still works, she is also writer and deputy editor for *area* magazine.

My Florence (but this is not an essay...)

Adolfo Natalini*

The geometrical plan of Florence by Federico Fantozzi shows the city in 1843, still enclosed by the walls built in 1333. As Edoardo Detti stated: "the circle that encloses the plan seems to define a form of unity and harmony that cannot be surpassed". The same map shows the overlaid plan by Poggi drawn up in 1865: the circle was no longer able to contain the city. The gardens inside the walls seemed crammed in, the new quarters of Barbano and Mattonaia had appeared, the "a new presumptuous boulevard" had replaced the walls which were still marked on the map, and the new quarters built outside the walls had already been traced. South of the Arno, the Viale dei Colli formed a winding avenue through the various sections of the city. Later the City Centre was gutted "to be restored to a new life", and new quarters were built on the outskirts that were far more senseless than the absurd interventions in the city centre. The viale remained as a strong reminder, marking the separation between the historic centre and the immediate outskirts. Nineteenth century architecture, largely embodied by Poggi's "Tuscan" style (aimed at transforming it into the style of the new nation) could have formed a decent model for successive interventions. But history was to take another course...

Those who walk around the city and its outskirts today ask themselves the question: where is the architecture of the last hundred years? Examples can be sought in various guides entitled *Modern Architecture in Florence*. The search is arduous, but with some effort, we are able to come up with a list: the Nervi Stadium, the Mazzoni and Michelucci Railway Stations, the Military Aviation Institute by Fagnoni (1930s), the reconstruction of the Santa Trinita Bridge by Gizdulich, la sala dei Primitivi in the Uffizi by Scarpa, Gardella and Michelucci, the Fondiaria Building by Giovannozzi (1950s), the Sorgane quarter by Savioli and Ricci, the Motorway Church of San Giovanni Battista by Michelucci, and the Nuova Italia building by Scarpa and Detti (1960s). After this period, the interventions were reduced to a minimum, architecture hidden or inserted between walls: interiors, stores, restoration projects.

The historic city seemed unable to reinvent itself. Architects were commissioned to create hidden interventions to avoid the suffocating web of regulations and restrictions aimed at protecting the city from an insane "glut" of building speculation, but, they suffocated any possibility of redemption through beautiful design...

Architecture was replaced by restoration, a necessary activity like maintenance and house cleaning, but hardly creative.

The new city (the expansion of the outskirts) was abandoned to soulless building construction as if it did not deserve good architecture, as if it was deprived of any hope of recovering a sense of identity.

And yet, Florence and its school of architecture have produced a number of extraordinarily talented architects over the past forty years, without having to always refer exclusively to the centenarian Michelucci, who by the way, was from Pistoia like me...

Flashes of creativity began to appear in the late Sixties, in conjunction with the flood of 1966 when Radical Architecture was born in Florence, (according to a catalogue by the Pompidou Centre, the most important Italian Avant-guarde movement in the latter half of the 20th century), together with groups like Archizoom, Superstudio and others.

The Eighties bought wonderful architects and designers such as David Palterer, Guglielmo Renzi, Guicciardini & Magni, Claudio Nardi, Elio Di Franco, Achille Michelizzi, Ipostudio, followed in the Nineties by Studio Archea.

All these architects built little or nothing in Florence; they were forced to carve out a space for themselves in parallel disciplines (design, interiors, communications) or had to create buildings in distant regions.

I still feel that Florence is more in need of good architecture today than architecture in the past was in need of Florence.

I have always loved this city, but I never felt appreciated in return.

Florence is a closed heartless city, always ready to crush others by making comparisons with its glorious past. It is a city that enjoys huge revenue because of its identity, but it is opposed to change and not generous in granting recognition.

Among the stone walls of Florence, you are made to feel like an intruder, an unwelcome visitor, or an accidental tourist. Its monuments fight a geometrical battle against one another and against any newcomer. Florence is crushed by the shadow of its famous dome.

I wanted to be a Florentine architect, but I never succeeded, and I was forced to accept opportunities to design buildings in other cities and other nations. In every place, I tried to learn a language that allowed me to communicate through architecture appropriate to the sense of place.

From Florence, I learnt a great deal on measurement, proportion, and scale, but also on the need to not stand out through diversity.

* Adolfo Natalini is full professor at the Florence Faculty of Architecture. In 1966 he founded Superstudio, initiator of the so-called "Radical Architecture" movement. Since 1991, he and his firm, Natalini Architetti, (Adolfo and Fabrizio Natalini) have reconstructed urban areas in Italy, Germany, and Holland.

Forte di Belvedere
Giardino di Boboli
Palazzo Pitti
Santo Spirito
Ponte Vecchio
Museo Bardini

Palazzo Vecchio
Giotto's
Bell Tower
Cathedral
Florence
Law Courts
San Lorenzo
Gallerie degli Uffizi
Museo Galileo

Santa Croce
Pazzi Chapel
Synagogue
Central National Library

© Neri Casamonti
Artemio Franchi Municipal Stadium
La Nazione
State Archives Building

Strategies for visiting Florence

In order to see all the major sights of Florence, visitors should calculate at least three or four days. The buildings described in this guide have been divided into three itineraries, and each one requires at least a whole day. For the historic city centre itinerary alone, we would recommend at least two days; this route includes many famous museums and some time should be dedicated to internal visits. The historic centre can be easily visited on foot, while we advise visitors to take public transport or a bicycle for the other two itineraries.

<u>Itinerary A | Historic Centre</u>
This itinerary begins symbolically with the **Santa Maria Novella Station/01**, the arrival point for visitors to Florence. From here one can continue to the historic centre or take public transport to follow one of the other itineraries. The pedestrian area of the city centre starts from **Piazza del Duomo /11** continues to Piazza della Repubblica, Piazza della Signoria (**Palazzo Vecchio - Uffizi Museum/28**) until it reaches **Palazzo Pitti/31.** This itinerary is enclosed by the ring roads constructed on the perimeter formerly occupied by the 16th century city walls. The historic centre is famous for its cultural monuments of enormous value, especially the museums and religious buildings, that include the **Uffizi Museum/28**, the **Museo dell'Opera del Duomo/12**, the **Museo degli Innocenti/17**, the **Complesso Mediceo Laurenziano/13**, **Basilica of Santa Croce/23** as well as the iconic symbols of the city and its moment of glory, the Renaissance. We invite visitors to discover the other side of the Arno, crossing its bridges, from the famous **Ponte Vecchio/31** to the more recent bridges like the **Amerigo Vespucci Bridge/08** and **Ponte alle Grazie/25**.
This strong historic context also includes important modern buildings, like the **Ex Bica Office Building/15** and the **Post and Telegraph Provincial Headquarters/19**, as well as more recent interventions to convert old buildings for new purposes, like the **Mercato Centrale Firenze /14** and the **Restoration of the ex Murate prison/22**.

<u>Itinerary B | Florence North-West</u>
This itinerary covers the western area outside the ring roads and includes the Fortezza da Basso, the important trade fair and events centre. Within its grounds is the **Spadolini Pavilion/36,** and the gardens also lead to the Parco delle Cascine; at the entrance is the **Opera Theatre/53** designed by ABDR Architetti Associati. Inside the park is the **Military Aviation Institute/52** designed by Raffaello Fagnoni. Nearby is the large complex of the **ex Tobacco Manufacturing Plant/58** which is currently part of an important redevelopment project. The itinerary covers quite a large area and visitors can take a tram as far as the **Scandicci Civic Centre/51** with the

current line, and when the last two sections have been completed, the line will continue through to the **Careggi Hospital entrance /40** and the **Novoli Quarter/59**. This "quarter" was the object of a vast transformation in the late nineties, with the creation of the Parco di San Donato, shopping centres and a university campus. This itinerary includes another university campus in Sesto Fiorentino, home to the **Florence University Incubator/43**. In this area, to the north of Florence, there is an unusual church designed by yet another famous architect, Giovanni Michelucci: the **Church of San Giovanni Battista, called "Chiesa dell'Autostrada"/45**.

Itinerary C | Florence South-East

Like the North/West itinerary, this tour also covers a large area and visitors need to take public transport. Again, it begins from the zone near the ring roads as far as the **Autostrada del Sole Acoustic Barriers/84** designed by Archea Associati. The itinerary starts with an important work by Italo Gamberini, the **State Archives Building/63**, then continues to include a second building by the same architect, the **RAI Headquarters/73**. Proceeding along the Viale dei Colli, after passing piazzale Michelangelo and its breath-taking panorama of the city, is one of the ancient religious and artistic icons of Florence, the **Abbey of San Miniato al Monte/80**. While in this area, it would be a pity not to visit one of the masterpieces if 1930s architecture, the **Artemio Franchi Municipal Stadium/68** by Pierluigi Nervi, with its modern helical stairways and the large cantilevered roof over the terraces. This itinerary also proposes several examples of renowned 1960s architecture, like the **Monterinaldi Residential Complex/69** by Leonardo Ricci, the **Apartment Building in Via Piagentina/72** and **Villa Bayon /81** by Leonardo Savioli and the **Sorgane Quarter/77**, a combined project by the two architects.

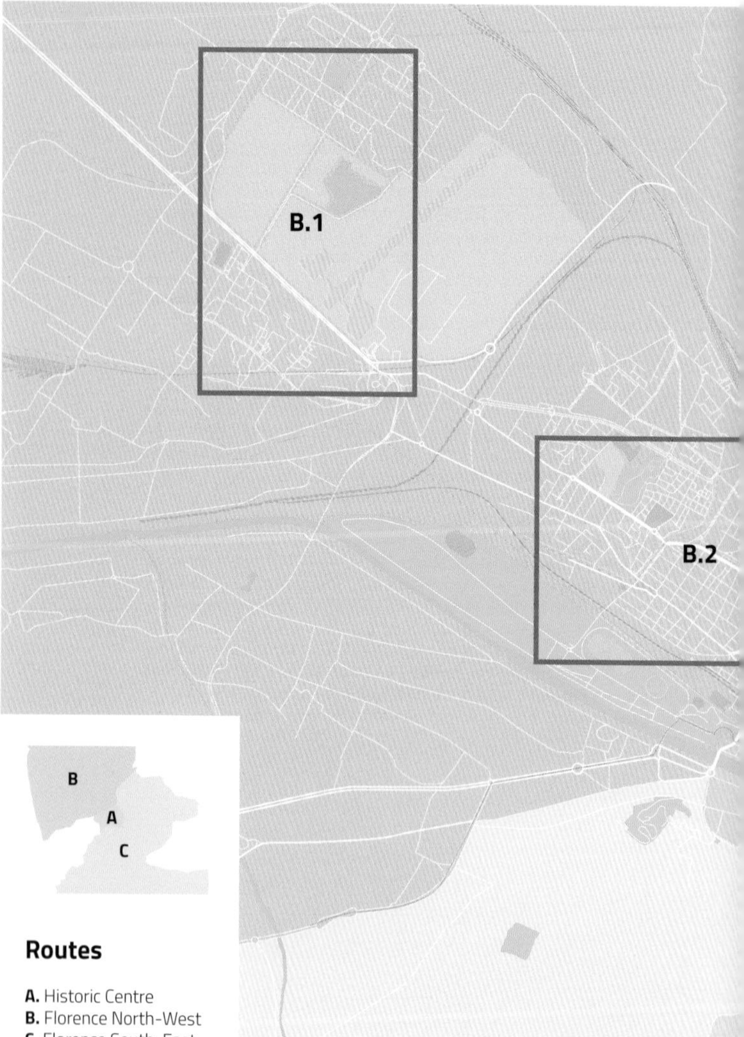

Routes

A. Historic Centre
B. Florence North-West
C. Florence South-East

A.1
A.2
C.

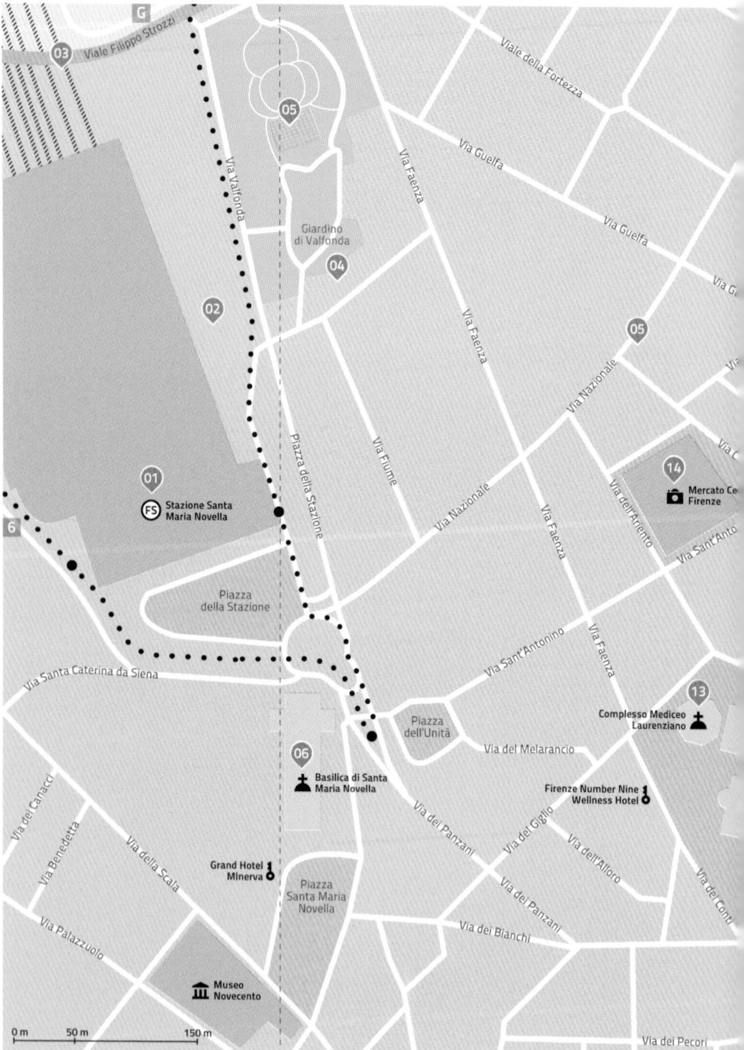

G
03
Viale Filippo Strozzi
05
Viale della Fortezza
Via Guelfa
Via Faenza
Via Valfonda
Giardino di Valfonda
04
02
Via Gu
05
Via Nazionale
01
Stazione Santa Maria Novella
6
Piazza della Stazione
Via Fiume
Via Nazionale
14
Mercato Ce Firenze
Via dell'Ariento
Via Sant'Anto
Piazza della Stazione
Via Sant'Antonino
Via Faenza
Via Santa Caterina da Siena
13
Complesso Mediceo Laurenziano
Piazza dell'Unità
Via del Melarancio
06
Basilica di Santa Maria Novella
Firenze Number Nine Wellness Hotel
Via dei Canacci
Via Benedetta
Via della Scala
Via dei Panzani
Via del Giglio
Via dell'Alloro
Grand Hotel Minerva
Piazza Santa Maria Novella
Via dei Panzani
Via dei Conti
Via Palazzuolo
Via dei Bianchi
Museo Novecento
0 m
50 m
150 m
Via dei Pecori

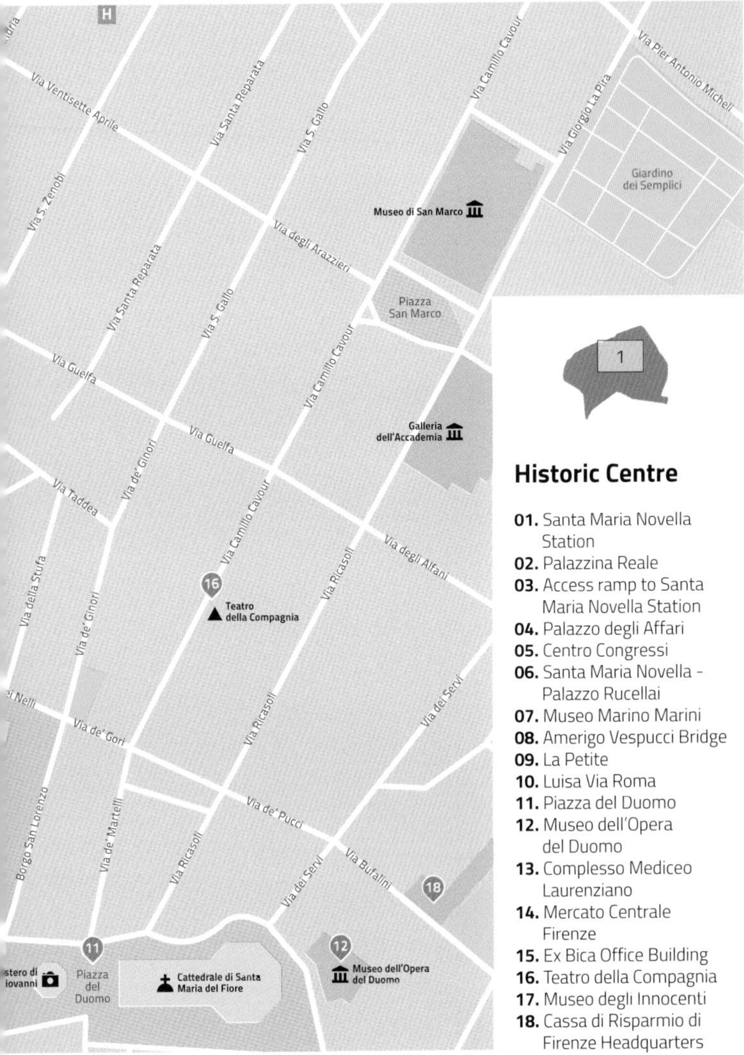

Historic Centre

01. Santa Maria Novella Station
02. Palazzina Reale
03. Access ramp to Santa Maria Novella Station
04. Palazzo degli Affari
05. Centro Congressi
06. Santa Maria Novella - Palazzo Rucellai
07. Museo Marino Marini
08. Amerigo Vespucci Bridge
09. La Petite
10. Luisa Via Roma
11. Piazza del Duomo
12. Museo dell'Opera del Duomo
13. Complesso Mediceo Laurenziano
14. Mercato Centrale Firenze
15. Ex Bica Office Building
16. Teatro della Compagnia
17. Museo degli Innocenti
18. Cassa di Risparmio di Firenze Headquarters

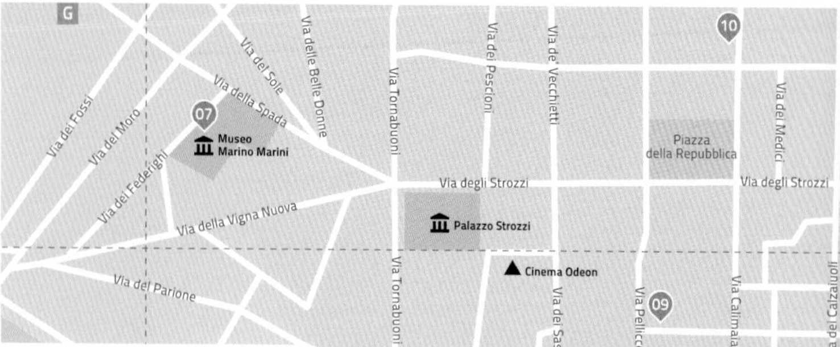
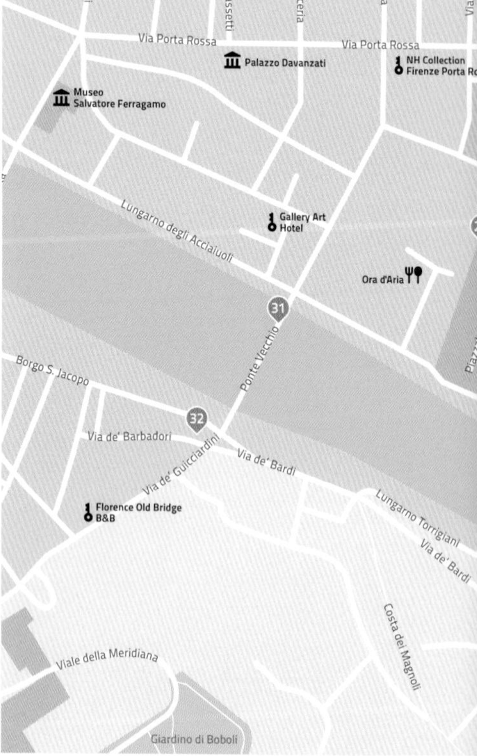

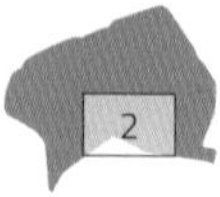

Historic Centre

19. Post and Telegraph Provincial Headquarters
20. Plesso di Santa Teresa - University of Architecture
21. La Nazione Headquarters
22. Restoration of the ex Murate prison
23. Basilica of Santa Croce
24. Central National Library
25. Ponte alle Grazie
26. Museo Galileo
27. Loggia del Grano and ex Capitol Renovation
28. Palazzo Vecchio - Uffizi Museum
29. Scala di Ponente - New Uffizi Extension
30. Sale dei Primitivi
31. Ponte Vecchio - Vasari Corridor - Palazzo Pitti
32. Ponte Vecchio area reconstruction
33. Church of Santo Spirito
34. Piedibus Project
35. Casa della Finestra

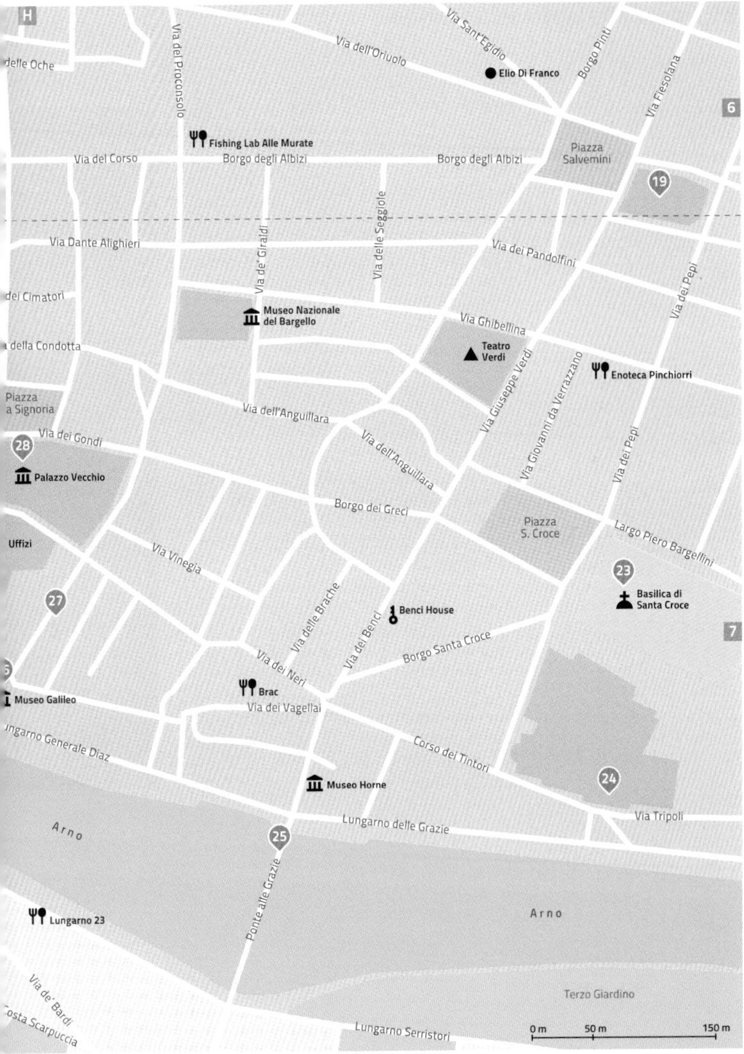
H
delle Oche
Via del Proconsolo
Via dell'Oriuolo
Via Sant'Egidio
Elio Di Franco
Borgo Pinti
Via Fiesolana
6
Fishing Lab Alle Murate
Via del Corso
Borgo degli Albizi
Borgo degli Albizi
Piazza Salvemini
19
Via delle Seggiole
Via de' Giraldi
Via Dante Alighieri
Via dei Pandolfini
Via dei Pepi
dei Cimatori
Museo Nazionale del Bargello
Via Ghibellina
della Condotta
Teatro Verdi
Enoteca Pinchiorri
Via Giuseppe Verdi
Via Giovanni da Verrazzano
Piazza a Signoria
Via dell'Anguillara
Via dei Gondi
28
Via dell'Anguillara
Via dei Pepi
Palazzo Vecchio
Borgo dei Greci
Piazza S. Croce
Largo Piero Bargellini
Uffizi
Via Vinegia
23
Basilica di Santa Croce
27
Via delle Brache
Benci House
Via dei Benci
7
Borgo Santa Croce
Via dei Neri
Brac
Museo Galileo
Via dei Vagellai
Lungarno Generale Diaz
Corso dei Tintori
Museo Horne
24
Lungarno delle Grazie
Via Tripoli
Arno
25
Ponte alle Grazie
Lungarno 23
Arno
Via de' Bardi
Costa Scarpuccia
Terzo Giardino
Lungarno Serristori
0 m
50 m
150 m

01. Santa Maria Novella Station

Piazza della Stazione
50123, Florence

January - December
Mon - Sun / 6 am - 9 pm

+39 055 2352190

www.
firenzesantamarianovella.it

T1 > Alamanni Stazione

6/11/14/17 > Stazione Arrivi
1/2/6/11/14/17/23 > Stazione Nazionale
6/11/12/17/22/23/36/37/C2/D > Stazione Scalette
22/C1/C2 > Stazione Via Panzani

Since the 19th century station was considered inadequate, and after the unsuccessful project by Mazzoni in 1931, a national competition was launched in 1932; it was won by the so-called "Gruppo Toscano".
Considered one of the best expressions of 20th century Italian Rational architecture, the station is in sharp contrast with the medieval Basilica of Santa Maria Novella. Although on one hand, the proximity of the two buildings provoked considerable discussion, on the other, certain respective elements were appreciated: the compact horizontal structure was not conflictual with the vertical Gothic architecture of the Basilica, while at the same time, the use of similar sandstone created a connection between the two buildings.
The compact stone façade is interrupted by the wide, steel-edged, glass cascade over the ticket sales area and the office space windows overlooking Via Valfonda. These are framed in white Travertine stone, also present on the façade in Via Alamanni. The internal architecture is composed of sleek lines and open spaces, like the ticket sales area and the end gallery, both lit with overhead glazed panels; this is combined with strong design that integrates different marble materials. Also worth noting is the attention paid to details such as the wood and steel furnishings, and art works by Ottone Rosai and Mario Romoli.

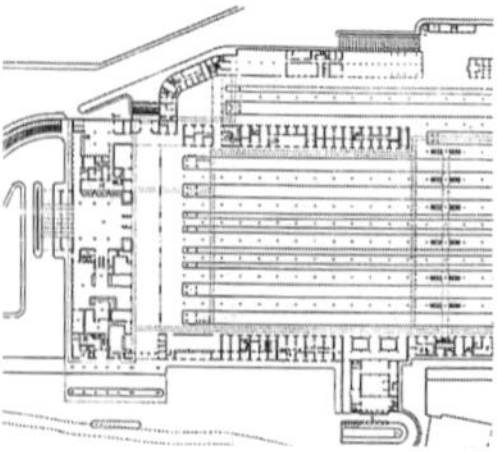

architects
Gruppo Toscano: Pier Niccolò Berardi, Nello Baroni, Italo Gamberini, Sarre Guarnieri, Leonardo Lusanna, Giovanni Michelucci

type
railway station

construction
1932-1935

02. Palazzina Reale

Piazza della Stazione 50
50123, Florence

January - December
Mon - Sun / 8 am - 1 am

+39 055 2645114
marketing@realefirenze.it
www.realefirenze.it

T1 > Alamanni Stazione

6/11/14/17 >
Stazione Arrivi
1/2/6/11/14/17/23
> Stazione Nazionale

Conceived in 1932 as part of the project for the Santa Maria Novella Station, and originally destined for the king to rest while travelling, in 1934, this building was radically redesigned to its current architectural form. The chief architects, Giovanni Michelucci, and other Gruppo Toscano members such as Italo Gamberini, supervised the construction until its inauguration on October 30, 1935.
This pure simple design is enhanced with prestige materials such as oak, walnut, glass and stucco, alongside exquisite marbles: pale pink for the external façades and dark green Alpine, white Carrara, Levanto and Castelpoggio red, beige Pavonazzo d'Arni and pale alabaster for the interiors.
Today the building is the headquarters of the Order of Architects of Florence, and also houses a café. The building can be accessed from the railway platform and from the principal entrance on the principle façade in via Valfonda. Externally, a large open space is defined on one side by an exedra, surrounded by walls with paraste and enhanced with a long central pool overlooked by a group sculpture by Italo Griselli depicting *The Arno and its Valley*. The heart of the building is the royal salon, with its ten-metre ceiling, the total height of the building; this is enclosed between two atriums and the private chambers of the king and his ministers with personal bathrooms.

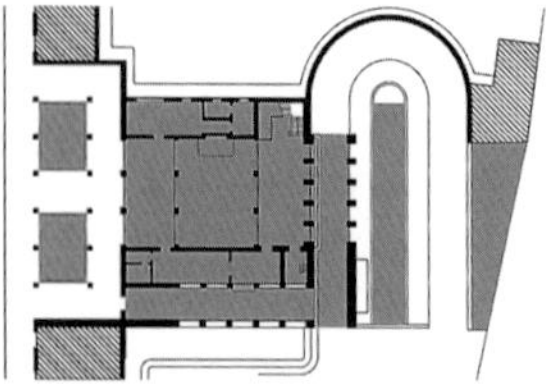

architects
Giovanni Michelucci

type
coffee bar, offices

construction
1934-1935

03. Access ramp to Santa Maria Novella Station

Piazzale Montelungo
50123, Florence

January - December
Mon - Sun / 6 am - 9 pm

+39 055 2352190

www.
firenzesantamarianovella.it

T1 > Alamanni Stazione

2/4/28/54 > Piazza Monte Lungo Firenze

For the World Cup Football Championships held in Italy in 1990, the Florence Railways Department decided to carry out improvement and redevelopment work on the city's stations. The Santa Maria Novella Station required an entrance on the Fortezza da Basso side because of the vast parking area in the vicinity. The entrance was designed as a long pedestrian ramp leading from the lower Fortezza level up to the platforms. The ramp crosses viale Strozzi with a pedestrian bridge that opens up to become a large hall and observation area. The bridge is covered with a sloped skylight roof, enclosed on each side by two brick towers recalling the context of the nearby Fortezza da Basso. These towers bear the truss beams which support the bridge. The flooring and parapets are all in brick. The parapets are punctuated with recessed lighting, while artificial light floods down from overhead in the bridge section. Steel was another high-impact material used for the bridge truss beams, recalling the design of railway bridges.

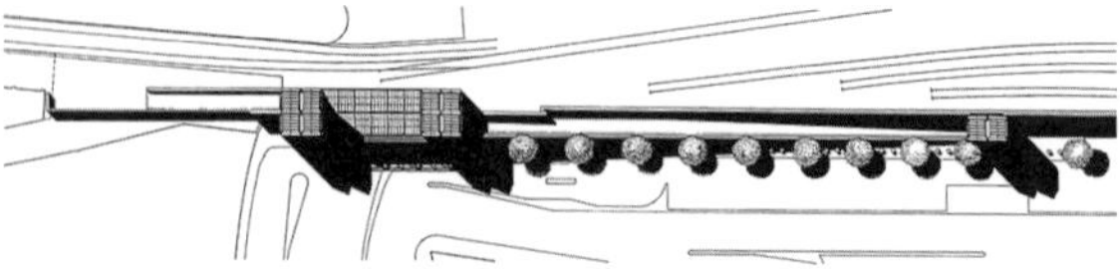

architects
Gae Aulenti,
Bianca Ballestrero

type
infrastructure

construction
1989-1990

04. Palazzo degli Affari

Piazza Adua 1
50123, Florence

external viewing only

+39 055 49721
info@firenzefiera.it
www.firenzefiera.it

6/11/14/17 > Stazione Arrivi
1/2/6/11/14/17/23 > Stazione Nazionale

The Palazzo degli Affari, near the Santa Maria Novella Railway Station in Florence, is set opposite the Palazzo dei Congressi, with which it shares the park space of Villa Vittoria. With the Fortezza da Basso, these buildings make up the Firenze Fiera congress and exhibition centre.
The volume of each level is reduced in size as it rises; this lightens the massive effect and provides a sense of continuation with other buildings in the surrounding historical centre. The façade also forms a contrasting element in comparison to traditional architecture: the prefabricated elements have a curved plinth design and perform a static function; the pseudo-inverted-arch design over-turns the canons of classical architecture. Light glass walls on the ground floor in Piazza Adua form a contrast with the mass of the upper floors, punctuated by embrasure-type openings. The prefabricated façade elements in white concrete, crushed stone and marble inert materials, are cleanly integrated with the horizontal structure: a prefabricated steel slab that contains all power and water installations.

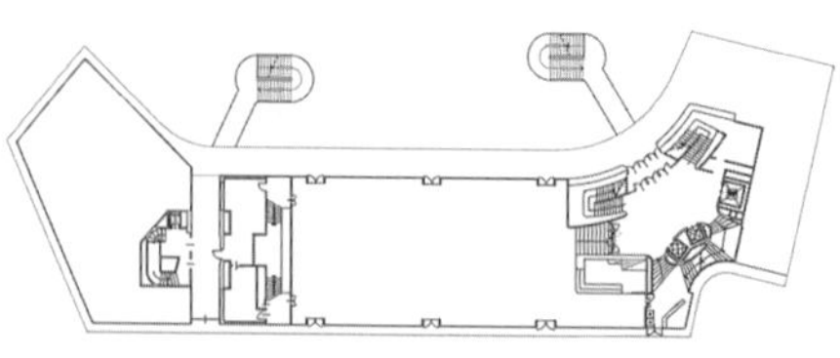

© Firenze Fiera

architects
Pierluigi Spadolini

type
offices, exhibition centre

construction
1968-1973

05. Centro Congressi

Piazza Adua 1, Via Valfonda 1, Viale Filippo Strozzi 2
50123, Florence

external viewing only

+39 055 49721
info@firenzefiera.it
www.firenzefiera.it

6/11/14/17 >
Stazione Arrivi
1/2/6/11/14/17/23
> Stazione Nazionale

Villa Vittoria, the focal point of the Florence Congress Centre, is a nineteenth century palace designed by Poggi's students. In the Sixties, the villa was chosen to host congresses and exhibitions, and underwent considerable restructuration work. Spadolini resolved the problem of adding an auditorium by building an integrated, communicating structure, but completely separate and distinct from the existing villa. The congress hall is built partially below ground but is visible from the gardens that suggest its shape: an open-air theatre acts as the roof over the congress hall and its curved lines trace paths through the green spaces. The congress hall level has access to the gardens through pedestrian passages and ramps in the lawn areas.
The hall structure has a strong plastic design, built in reinforced concrete cast on site, with helicoidal galleries and walkways that define the single and double floors. The hall, 37 metres in diameter with seating for 1,000, is covered with a large ring of prestressed, reinforced concrete, supported in four points. The concave roofing was built using a reticular truss beam structure, and the ceiling covered with triangular, spherically curved elements to provide top quality acoustics.

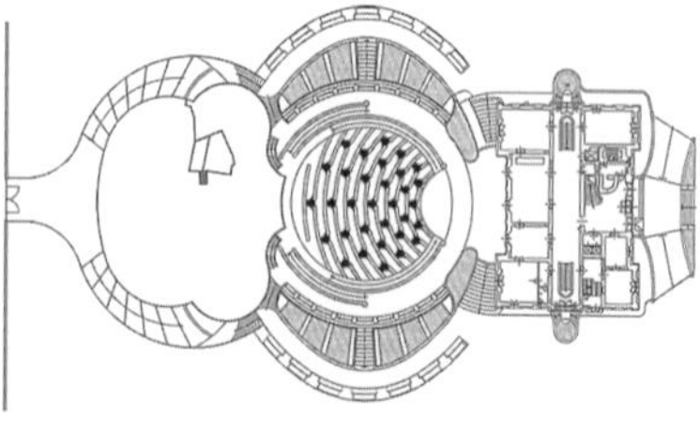

architects
Pierluigi Spadolini

type
auditorium, offices

construction
1963-1964

06. Santa Maria Novella - Palazzo Rucellai

Santa Maria Novella:
Piazza Santa Maria Novella 18
Palazzo Rucellai:
Via della Vigna Nuova 18
50123, Florence

Santa Maria Novella:
open to the public
+39 055 219257
info@smn.it
www.smn.it

Palazzo Rucellai:
external viewing only
+39 055 2645910
info@isiflorence.org
www.isiflorence.org

Santa Maria Novella:
22/C1/C2 > Stazione Via Panzani
Palazzo Rucellai:
6/11 > Vigna Nuova

The Dominican Basilica of Santa Maria Novella (photo), built in the piazza of the same name between the 13th and 14th centuries, was constructed over the pre-existent Church of Santa Maria delle Vigne. The current building has a Latin Cross layout with three naves and a transept, cross-vaulted ceilings, and lancet windows. However the Gothic elements are tempered by the massive stone architectural structure without the traditional Gothic height. The façade is faced in multi-coloured marble, which remained uncompleted at the first level of the tombs until the 1450s, when Giovanni Rucellai commissioned its completion by Leon Battista Alberti in 1470. He combined the previous Medieval style with Renaissance design based on ancient models, such as the triumphal entrance arch, the tympanum, and the proportional ratios based on the square.
During the same period and in the same area, Giovanni Rucellai also commissioned Alberti to design the façade for Palazzo Rucellai, his loggia, and the Rucellai chapel in the current Museo Marino Marini (07). The palace was internally reconstructed by Rossellino by uniting several residences, and was finished with the application (suddenly interrupted on one side), of a facade-manifesto of Alberti's architectural style, based on three superimposed classical orders, Tuscan, Ionic and Corinthian, in a series of identical bays, except for the larger entrance openings flanked by street benches whose stone backs imitate Roman reticulated work. The same architectural pattern is repeated a few metres away, in the chapel, in a tomb designed to interpret the Holy Sepulchre in Renaissance style.

architects
Santa Maria Novella:
Fra Sisto da Firenze, Fra Ristoro da Campi, Fra Jacopo Talenti, Leon Battista Alberti
Palazzo Rucellai: Bernardo Rossellino, Leon Battista Alberti

type
church, multi-purpose building

construction
Santa Maria Novella:
1240 - 1470 circa
Palazzo Rucellai:
1455 - 1470 circa

07. Museo Marino Marini

Piazza di San Pancrazio
50123, Florence

January - December
Wed - Fri / 10 am - 1 pm
Sat - Mon / 10 am - 7 pm
Tue / closed

+39 055 219432
info@museomarinomarini.it
www.museomarinomarini.it

6/11 > Vigna Nuova

This Museum was created following the conversion of the former Church of San Pancrazio; the architectural design of the complex was centred around the works to be exhibited. The project was decided by the Florence city council in its desire to give new life to the former church and to find a suitable setting for the collection of Marini's works, donated to the city in 1980. The museum now occupies this historic building which was extended considerably, undergoing many changes over the centuries. After its deconsecration in 1808, the building was used for a wide range of civic purposes.
From the entrance, the transparent counter façade reveals the cleverly structured interior which, according to Marini's wishes, is composed of large open spaces, natural light, and different viewing points for the various works. The space has been designed with walkways and galleries at various levels around the vast open central space under the transparent roof set on 19th century steel beams. Modern structures and materials – exposed reinforced concrete, steel, glass and wood – contrast with ancient elements like the *Gloria Celeste* fresco by Sigismondo Betti in the lowered dome over the altar area, and the columns on the façade, the historic filter by Alberti between the nave and the Rucellai chapel made accessible from the museum in 2012, moved here at the beginning of the 19th century.

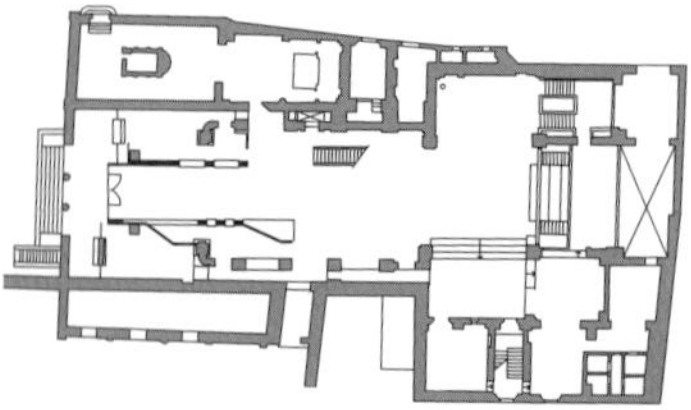

architects
Bruno Sacchi, Lorenzo Papi

type
museum

construction
1982-1986

08. Amerigo Vespucci Bridge

Ponte Amerigo Vespucci
50123, Florence

open to the public

6/12/36/37/
C3/D > S. Rosa Sn
C3 > Ponte Vespucci

The need for a bridge between the new Cascine district and the old quarter of San Frediano became obvious at the end of the nineteenth and beginning of the twentieth centuries. Following the destruction of Florence's bridges during the withdrawal of Nazi troops in August 1944, a temporary passage was built in 1950.

In 1952, the Comune held a competition for a new bridge, built between 1954 and 1957, and based on the design by architects Enzo Gori, Giorgio Giuseppe Gori, and Ernesto Nelli, and the engineer, Riccardo Morandi. The bridge features a thin flat arch, with a counterweighted, triple-span, prestressed deck structure. It does not reflect the usual arched shape of Florentine bridges, but maintains greater linearity and continuity with the banks of the Arno. The overall effect is one of a continuous single span paved with porphyry blocks resting on two limestone-faced piers to reflect the Florentine urban fabric. The linear parapet is in chased, rectangular section steel. The design also includes the lighting installation composed of strip lighting down the dividing line between the two carriageways.

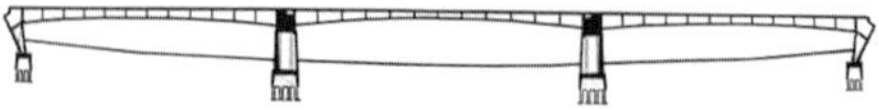

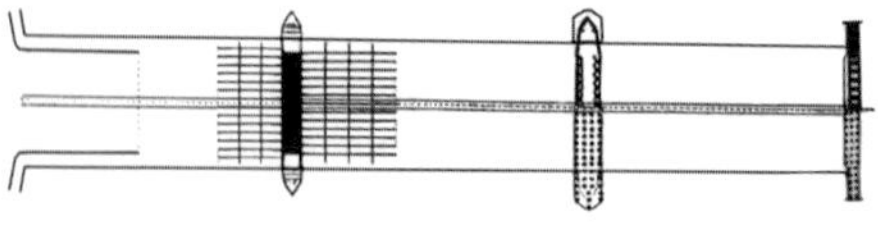

© Neri Casamonti

architects
Enzo Gori, Giorgio Giuseppe Gori, Ernesto Nelli, Riccardo Morandi

type
bridge

construction
1952 competition
1954-1957 construction

09. La Petite

Via Pellicceria 30
50123, Florence

open to the public

+39 055 212701

www.lapetitefirenze.it

C2 > Porta Rossa

The La Petite cocktail bar and restaurant was converted by joining two adjacent 19th century buildings: a store and a restaurant.
The architects, Javier Deferrari and Lavinia Modesti, eliminated all the former superstructures and carried out a complete renovation, re-arranging the layout, introducing new materials, furnishings, and lighting, to increase the luminosity. The two levels are connected by a staircase positioned near the entrance, which forms the spatial core and focal point. The staircase design, initially straight, then fan-shaped, reduces the occupied space, while the alternating steel rod and leather strip structure enables customers to move easily between floors. The slim wooden stair treads accentuate the light transparent effect, together with the fine leather strips, that give a vibrant touch to the stair railing.
The cocktail-bar is located on the ground floor, with the restaurant upstairs.
The bar space is enriched with a wall sculpture in pale travertine stone adding extra light: a tribute to the artist Costantino Nivola and Florentine stone façades, reinterpreted with a composition of prismatic stone elements that, when placed alongside one another at different angles, create a vibrant effect that changes with the light.

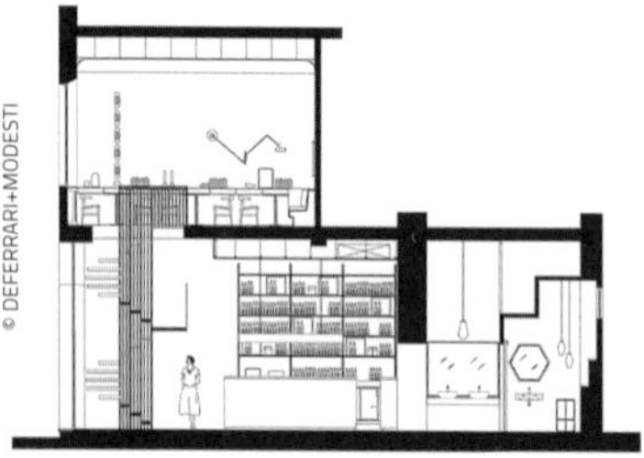

architects
DEFERRARI+MODESTI

type
bar, restaurant

construction
2012-2013

10. Luisa Via Roma

Via Roma 19r/21r
50123, Florence

January - December
Mon - Sat / 10.30 am - 7.30 pm
Sun / 11 am - 7.30 pm

+39 055 9064116

www.luisaviaroma.com

C1/C2 > Roma Duomo

Designed by Claudio Nardi back in 1984, the boutique was renovated in 2008 by the same architect, using concrete, steel, Corian, and tempered structural glass. The minimalist and subtly sophisticated interior is laid out over three floors, arranged for store display, but also for events, exhibitions and fashion shows. The three floors are connected by an elevator and two glass staircases. The main ground-floor space it lit from above through the tempered glass floor of the large terrace on the first floor, supported by eight glass beams; the terrace is linked to the café space. The plain, unadorned, exposed concrete shell with its tectonic effect, is divided into a series of spaces in a play of transparency, with the use of glass walls and led lighting designed to create a translucent light. This permits functional variations and transformations to create different backdrops. Shelving becomes bench seating, windows are transformed into display cases, mobile display elements and sliding doors change the scenes. These elements are associated with a sophisticated hidden cable system controlling a myriad of hi-tech screens, which can be positioned in different ways and areas for video screening and web link-up.

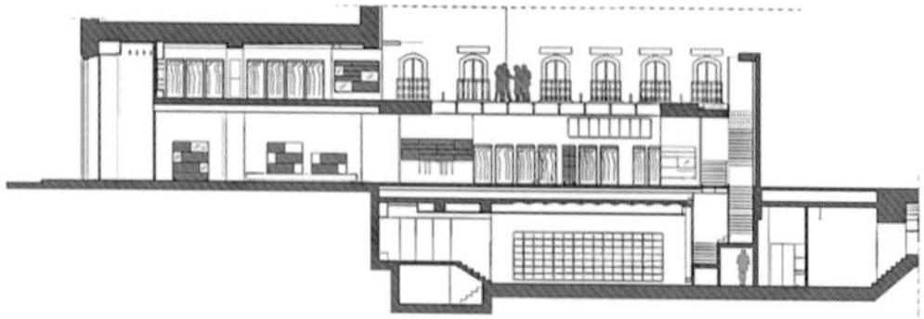

architects
Claudio Nardi Architects

type
retail

construction
2007-2008

11. Piazza del Duomo

Piazza del Duomo
50122, Florence

open to the public

+39 055 2302885
opera@operaduomo.firenze.it
www.
ilgrandemuseodelduomo.it

C1 > Studio
C1/C2 > Roma Duomo

Piazza del Duomo houses the most important religious complex in Florence. Composed of the Cathedral of Santa Maria del Fiore, the Giotto bell tower, and the Baptistery of Saint John, the three devotional buildings are semantically united by their façades in white Carrara, green Prato and red Maremma marbles.

The Cathedral, is an imposing building composed of three naves; the central nave under the famous dome was begun in 1296 by Arnolfo di Cambio over the ruins of the ancient cathedral of Santa Reparata, which can be visited underground, below the present cathedral. The construction was transferred to Giotto in 1334, and then assigned to Talenti in 1350. Talenti modified the Arnolfo layout, proposing a new extended shape, including internal columns to support large ogival vaulted ceilings. In 1418, Brunelleschi began the construction of his dome; it became the symbol of the city and a subject of research for its innovative constructive technique. The double self-supporting shell system eliminated the traditional support frame structure. Although it was consecrated in 1436, the façade, by De Fabris, was not was completed until 1887. On the right is the bell tower designed by Giotto, but which he built only to the first level; it was later completed by Andrea Pisano followed by Talenti.

The origins of the Baptistery, with its octagonal floorplan and eight-sectioned dome, are uncertain; it is thought it was built between Paleo Christian times and the first millennium. The external facing was applied between the 12th and 13th centuries and exquisite mosaic work decorates the interior. Both the northern and eastern doors, the so-called "Gates of Paradise", were created following the famous competition held in 1401, in which Brunelleschi lost to the winner, Ghiberti.

© Neri Casamonti

architects
Cathedral: Arnolfo di Cambio, Francesco Talenti, Filippo Brunelleschi, Emilio De Fabris
Bell tower: Giotto, Andrea Pisano, Francesco Talenti

type
public space

construction
Cathedral: 1296-1436 (façade 1884-1887)
Bell tower: 1298-1359
Baptistery: 4th-5th century or 11th century (uncertain date)

12. Museo dell'Opera del Duomo

Piazza del Duomo 9
50122, Florence

January - December
Mon - Sun / 9 am - 7.30 pm
closed first Tuesday of the month

+39 055 2302885
opera@operaduomo.firenze.it
www.
ilgrandemuseodelduomo.it

C2 > Oriuolo
C1/C2 > Proconsolo

Opened in 1891 for the exhibition of art works connected with the Cathedral, the current museum is the result of a renovation project curated by Timothy Verdon for the museum exhibits, and by Natalini, Guicciardini and Magni for the architectural design. Following the purchase in 1998 of the adjacent former Teatro degli Intrepidi, later used as a depot and garage, it was possible to expand the museum, doubling the surface to include 28 rooms spread over three floors. The main focus is concentrated on the vast theatrical space with its natural overhead lighting: entitled "del Paradiso", it is 36 metres long and 20 metres high. This height has permitted the construction of a life-size reproduction of the 14th century façade of the Cathedral, never completed, and demolished in 1587. The architectural structure is composed of alabaster dust and resin moulded over a steel frame, and based on the drawings by Bernardino Poccetti at the time of the demolition.
The complete renovation of the exhibition space, reconstruction work and extension of the entire museum also includes an entirely new layout and the creation of additional levels incorporating two more stairways in addition to the existing great staircase.

architects
Natalini Architetti, Guicciardini & Magni Architetti Studio Associato

type
museum

construction
2004-2015

13. Complesso Mediceo Laurenziano

Basilica and Laurentian Library: Piazza San Lorenzo 9
Medici Chapels: Piazza di Madonna degli Aldobrandini 6
50123, Florence

March - October
Mon - Sat / 10 am - 5 pm
Sun / 1.30 pm - 5.30 pm
November - February
Mon - Sat / 10 am - 5 pm
Sun / closed

+39 055 214042
segreteria@operamedicealaurenziana.org
www.operamedicealaurenziana.org

C1 > San Lorenzo

The Complex of San Lorenzo, composed of a Basilica, two cloisters, a library and the two Medici Chapels: the New Sacristy and the Princes' Chapel, is the result of centuries of construction under the patronage of the Medici family.

The church, with its Latin Cross layout, was designed by Brunelleschi to replace a former, older church. The Basilica and the Old Sacristy, on the left side of the transept, can be considered as examples of early Florentine Renaissance architecture with elements such as the serena stone structures flanked by white plaster walls, the mathematical proportions, and modularity inspired by ancient models. The façade, never realised, was the object of countless projects, first of all, that designed by Michelangelo between 1517 and 1520. He also designed the Laurentian Library and the New Sacristy, symmetrical with the Old Sacristy, but including new elements in the architecture and in the proportions in height. He also used white marble, in both architecture and sculpture. It was only in 1604 that work was finally begun on the Chapel of the Princes. The only example of Florentine Baroque architecture, it is composed of a large octagonal room, completely covered in "commesso" inlay work in pietra dura, and roofed with a frescoed dome, second in size only to that of Florence Cathedral.

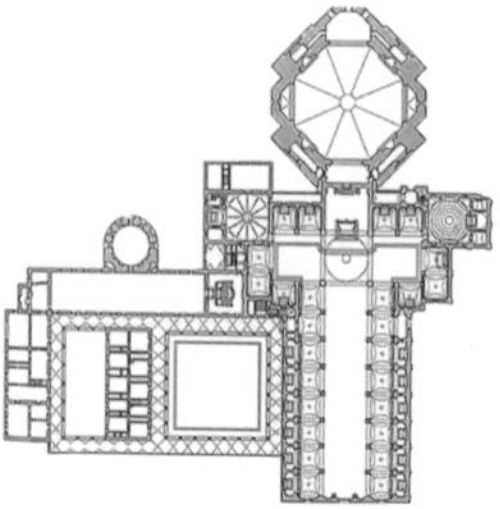

© Neri Casamonti

architects
Filippo Brunelleschi, Michelangelo Buonarroti, Giorgio Vasari, Bartolomeo Ammannati, Giovanni de' Medici, Matteo Nigetti

type
church, library

construction
1418-1962

14. Mercato Centrale Firenze

Via dell'Ariento, Piazza del Mercato Centrale
50123, Florence

January - December
Mon - Sun / 8 am - 12 pm

+39 055 2399798
info@mercatocentrale.it
www.mercatocentrale.it

1/2/6/11/14/ 17/23 > Stazione Nazionale
C1> San Lorenzo

The redevelopment of the first floor of the historic market of San Lorenzo created a new covered urban space in the centre of Florence. The cast iron and glass structure was built in the 1850s, modelled on the famous "Halles" market in Paris, as part of a modernising project when Florence was capital of Italy. This space was the basis for a new project: it combined architecture with food, creating a welcoming location to promote local traditional crafts and quintessential Tuscan wines and gastronomy. Food and beverage preparation, tastings, and sales points are all open to the public in a single large space where boutiques, aligned in a regular order, are integrated with the use of flexible mobile structures, open to passers-by. They are made of natural materials: wood, terracotta, rope, pigmented concrete.
This intervention did not require any radical building regulations or technology, which had previously been carried out in 2008. For functional reorganisation, the furnishings were made to measure and lit with large reed and wicker lampshades, accentuating the light airy effect of the 19th century cast iron elements.

© Archea Associati

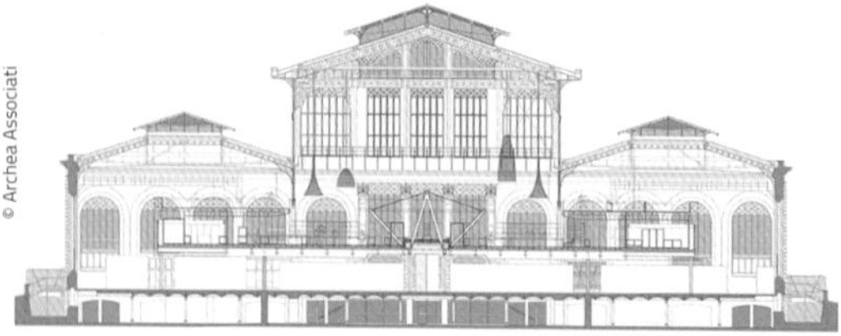

architects
Archea Associati

type
retail

construction
2014

15. Ex Bica Office Building

Via Nazionale 87-95
50123, Florence

external viewing only

1/2/6/11/14/17/23 >
Stazione Nazionale

Gamberini used great skill in balancing new technological architectural solutions with such a famous urban environment like the historic centre of Florence. It was, in fact, the first example of a curtain wall built in Florence. The façade, the result of advanced technological research, maintained the proportions, colours and themes that recalled Renaissance palaces. The protruding cornice is a clear example, although it was interpreted with the use of the cement-framed glass brick grid creating an elegant play of shadow on the façade.
The brise-soleil systems slide horizontally and protrude from the façade giving a three-dimensional effect. The strong horizontal elements like the brise-soleil, ribbon windows, and solid bands between floors, faced with gres bricks, are interrupted by the vertical lines of the window frames. This results in harmonised proportions inherited from Florentine Humanist building ideals.
Commenting on this design that won the In/Arch. Prize in 1963, Adalberto Libera wrote: "Gamberini is well-trained in his design, a conscientious professional in his construction; he believes in what he does, a man with a moral empire, a man who knows his work and who can pass on his knowledge".

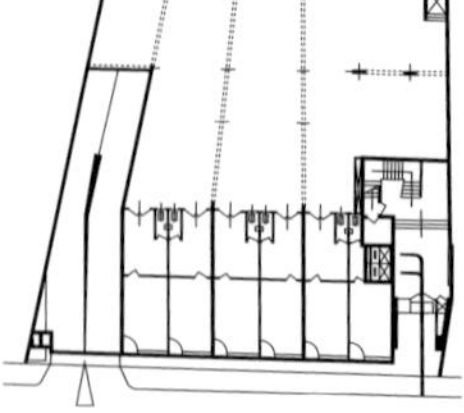

architects
Italo Gamberini

type
offices, retail

construction
1957-1959

16. Teatro della Compagnia

Via Camillo Cavour 50r
50121, Florence

open to the public

+39 055 268451
info@cinemalacompagnia.it
www.cinemalacompagnia.it

C1 > Cavour
14/23/C1 > Via De' Pucci

The building is located on a long narrow plot with the main entrance in Via Cavour, and a second access from a parallel street, Via Ricasoli. The floor plan is laid out in a longitudinal direction. The theatre is accessed through a small entrance on the main stone-faced façade, protected by a projecting shelter. Visitors proceed along a barrel-vaulted corridor with an octagonal ticket desk space and hexagonal bar area, seemingly carved out from the walls; this leads to the foyer, also with a barrel-vaulted ceiling. A lobby area acts as a filter to the stalls area and the two side staircases leading to the box seats. The theatre has a rectangular layout and because of its shape and materials, is conceived like an external space. The walls are faced with pink Santafiora stone finished with an entablature with a denticular cornice. The long walls are divided into four sections by pilasters and on the ground floor, are punctuated by porticos mounted with architraves, while on the upper floor, loggias with segmental arches enclose the boxes. Following the continuous theme, several blocks protrude from the stone wall facing, creating movement in perspective and improving theatre acoustics.
Beyond the proscenium is a large stage and full height stage tower.

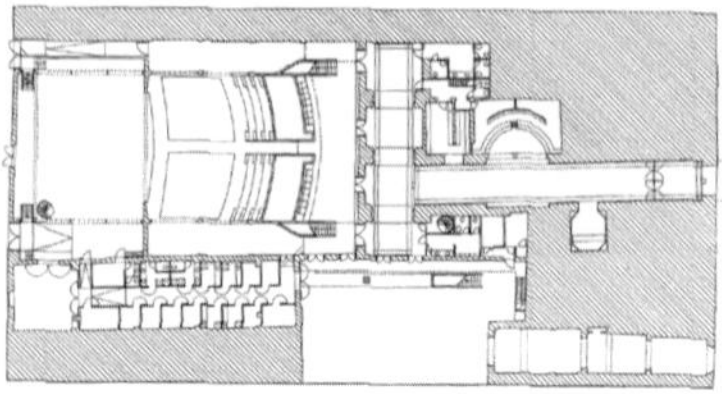

© Natalini Architetti

architects
Natalini Architetti

type
cinema, theatre

construction
1984-1987

17. Museo degli Innocenti

Piazza SS. Annunziata 13
50121, Florence

January - December
Mon - Sun / 10 am - 7 pm

+39 055 20371
info@istitutodeglinnocenti.it
www.istitutodeglinnocenti.it

6/14/19/
23/31 > Santissima Annunziata

This hospice was commissioned by the Silk Guild, Arte della Seta, at the beginning of the 15th century to care for abandoned children. It was designed by Filippo Brunelleschi in 1419, and continued its role as an orphanage for almost 600 years. The building still contains areas dedicated to children today.
The new museum, focused on art, architecture, history of childhood, and the rights of minors, is spread over a 1456 square metre exhibition space, with a further 1655 square metres assigned to temporary events linked with children's issues. The building also houses a literary café in the 15th century loggia, located inside a wood and glass structure that can be changed according to necessity, and that is independently accessible to the public even without museum tickets.
The architectural renovations included two new entrances in Piazza SS. Annunziata, with bronzed brass framing, plus an elevator and a steel and Matraia stone staircase connecting the five floors, including a basement not used previously.
The basement floor tells the history of the orphanage, the ground floor narrates the architectural evolution of the historic hospice, while the second floor, above the large portico, is dedicated to art history with works displayed on staggered, mobile panels hinged to the long curtain wall that conceals the electrical and technical installations.

© Ipostudio

architects
Ipostudio, Eutropia Architettura (café and children's museum)

type
museum

construction
2008-2016

18. Cassa di Risparmio di Firenze Headquarters

Via Bufalini 6
50121, Florence

January - December
Mon - Fri / 9 am - 7 pm
Sat - Sun / closed

+39 055 5384001
info@fondazionecrfirenze.it
www.fondazionecrfirenze.it

14/23/C1> Santa Maria Nuova

Between 1953 and 1957, Giovanni Michelucci worked on the architectural design and furnishing of the new headquarters of the Cassa di Risparmio di Firenze, which had been transferred from Palazzo Medici Riccardi to Palazzo Pucci in 1865. Since the reconstruction by Pasquale Faldi in 1886 was considered obsolete for the bank's needs, the Michelucci project was designed to blend architectural structures that were centuries apart.

The initial design for a façade set directly on the street was eliminated, and the layout was pivoted to face the rear, occupying a rectangular plot in a street perpendicular to via Bufalini. The complex is composed of two structures connected by an internal street which acts as a passage between both buildings; in the centre part, it forms a large gallery that gives access on the left, to four floors of office space with views over an internal garden; on the right is the public hall surrounded by wide balconies. The two long sides of the building have glazed façades, one overlooking the garden, with a modular metal grid system, and the other, to the east, with small, slightly projecting vaults forming a cornice.

The building was completely renovated between 2010 and 2013 to restore the original project; this included transparent glass partitions to reduce the visual impact on the original design.

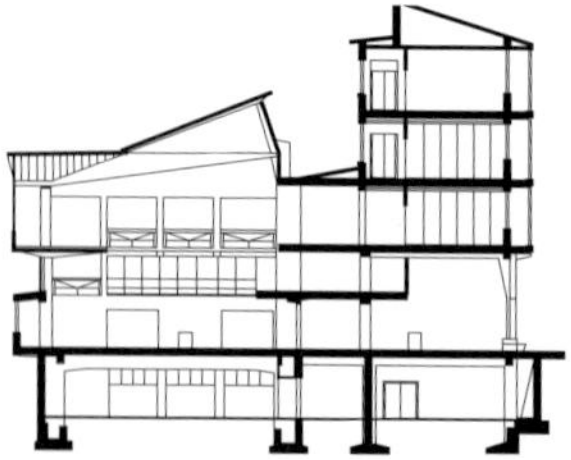

architects
Giovanni Michelucci / Progettisti Associati Annalisa Baracchi and Giuliano Galzigni (renovation)

type
offices

construction
1953-1957
2011-2013 (renovation)

19. Post and Telegraph Provincial Headquarters

Via Pietra Piana 84r
50121, Florence

January - December
Mon - Fri / 8.15 am - 7 pm
Sat / 8.15 am - 12.30 am
Sun / closed

+39 055 2612237

14/23/C1/C2 >
Salvemini

Built in the district of Santa Croce on a block demolished during the 1930s, the Post Office Building also includes open public spaces, offices and residential apartments. The façade features a staggered structure and recessed spaces, showing an attempt to merge with the surrounding urban fabric composed of different heights and architectural designs. The project shows the architect's reflection on urban streets, understood as connecting spaces and openings, and not as separations between buildings.
His desire to create important spatial relationships can be seen inside the light-filled layout of the public hall "piazza", and in the "street" parallel to Via Pietra Piana, marked by large columns and designed as an open seating space for public use. Overlooking this area are the stairs and upper floors.
Another feature is the choice of materials: San Giuliano limestone for the irregular ashlar stonework of the base, exposed reinforced concrete for the upper floors and ribbon windows framed in bronze anodised aluminium.

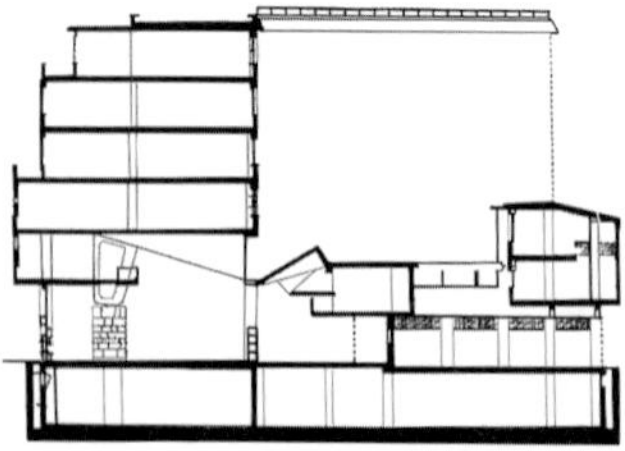

architects
Giovanni Michelucci

type
offices

construction
1959–1967

20. Plesso di Santa Teresa - University of Architecture

Via della Mattonaia 14
50122, Florence

open to the public

+39 055 2755410

www.architettura.unifi.it

C2/C3 > Annigoni
6/19/31 > D'Azeglio
6/14/19/23/31/
C2/C3 > Leopardi
Gramsci

The new university complex of Santa Teresa, that houses the faculty of architecture, is located in a former 17th century monastery designed by the architect, Giovanni Coccapani. In the 19th century, the convent was closed and converted to a prison facility. In 1985, the detainees were transferred to the new Sollicciano prison and the complex was assigned to the University of Florence.
Following an initial cell conversion to classrooms, a more radical transformation was necessary. The project began in 2005. The intervention by Breschistudio associati kept in mind the centuries-old, historical layering and decided to reveal the stratification, maintaining as much of the original structure as possible. On a functional level, the complex was divided into two large blocks, one dedicated to the Faculty of Architecture, and the other to the Department of Design. The first occupies the three blocks of the 19th century prison extensions, and the second occupies the core of the former convent. A new glazed building forms the distributive backbone of the entire complex. This structure forms a link between the three parallel buildings, Via della Mattonaia, and the two main blocks. There is also a new entrance where the new structure meets Via della Mattonaia.

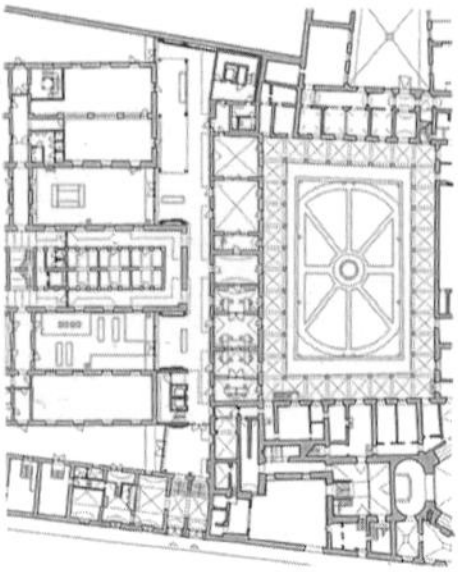

© Breschistudio associati

architects
Breschistudio associati

type
university

construction
2005-2016

21. La Nazione Headquarters

Viale della Giovine Italia 17
50121, Florence

external viewing only

+39 055 24991
segreteria.redazione.firenze@monrif.net
www.lanazione.it

8/13/14/23/31 > Giovine Italia
81/12 > Gioberti
C2/C3 > Annigoni

The Nazione newspaper complex comprises four buildings housing different departments: direction, editorial staff and production; it is located between the Santa Croce district and Piazza Beccaria. The building, designed by Spadolini, had to harmonise with the miscellaneous surrounding context including the Santa Verdiana complex, home to the Faculty of Architecture.
The orientation and height of the structures are designed to blend with the urban fabric based on the view seen from Piazzale Michelangelo: the buildings are laid out orthogonal to the large square to reduce visual impact to a minimum. The block overlooking Viale Giovine Italia houses the advertising department and several offices; the square building, opposite, houses the linotypes and printing presses; a rectangular structure, set in a more internal position, houses the direction, editorial staff, and more office spaces; the smallest building is home to the administration offices and an auditorium that faces Via Paolieri. One of the most characteristic aspects of Spadolini's design was the decision to use prefabricated elements on site. The façade is composed of standard 90 cm modules, precast and steam-cured on site and held together with tensioned cables.

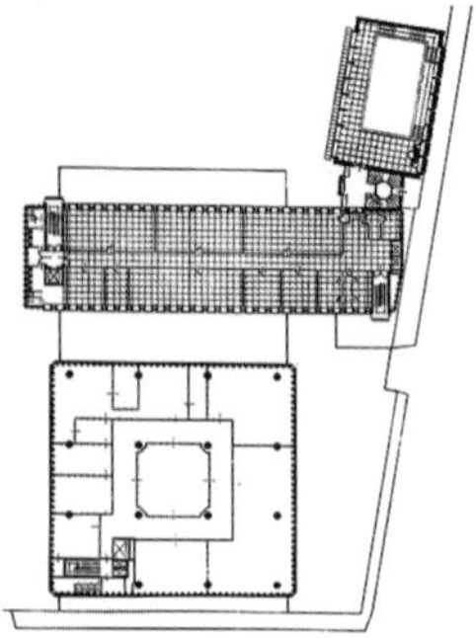

architects
Pierluigi Spadolini

type
offices

construction
1961-1966

22. Restoration of the ex Murate prison

Piazza della Madonna della Neve, Piazza delle Murate
50122, Florence

open to the public

www.lemurate.comune.fi.it

8/13/14/ 23/31 > Giovine Italia

This 15th century complex, now an important constructive and functional restoration project, was originally the convent of an enclosed order called "Murate" [behind closed walls], and later between 1883 and 1985, it became prison in Florence.
In 1997 the Comune allocated funding to transform the complex into an urban public housing block. The project was launched by a work team composed of technicians from various city council administration departments, and during the initial stage, of research scholars guided by Renzo Piano in his role as UNESCO ambassador for urbanism. The main reason behind the intervention was the desire to create layers of different functions to provide the diversified atmosphere typical of a vibrant contemporary urban centre. The restoration project allows the city to recover the use of an urban block, that since its construction in the 15th century, has never been accessible to the public; the ground floor level is now available for public use, never possible before. Today, the complex comprises 73 apartments for social housing (between 30 and 80 square metres), covered walkways, 800 square metres of office space, 560 square metres for workshops, a restaurant and a cafeteria, an area for advanced technology businesses and four auditoriums.

© Comune di Firenze

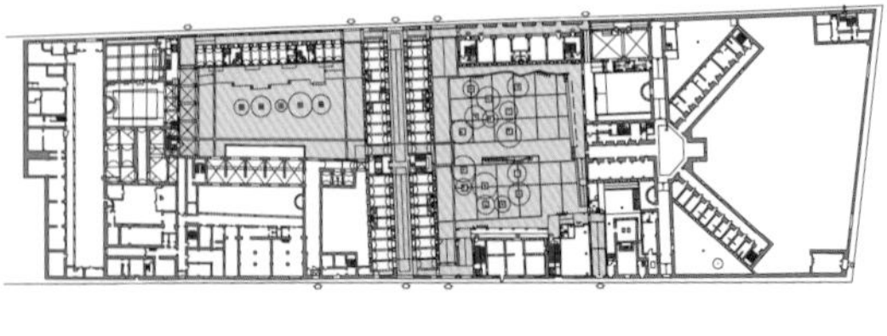

architects
Roberto Melosi, Mario Pittalis, Ufficio ERP del Comune di Firenze

type
residential, retail, offices, bar, restaurant

construction
1998-2007

23. Basilica of Santa Croce

Piazza Santa Croce 16
50122, Florence

open to the public

www.santacroceopera.it

C3 > Magliabechi
23/C1/C3 > Verdi

In 1294, on the opposite side of the city from the Dominican Basilica of Santa Maria Novella, the Franciscan order built the magnificent Basilica of Santa Croce, overlooking the piazza of the same name. Austere and simple, following Franciscan principles, the design has been traditionally attributed to Arnolfo di Cambio and was completed in the 19th century with a multi-coloured marble façade and Neo-gothic bell tower designed by Matas and Baccani. The Tau Cross layout is composed of three naves divided by octagonal stone columns supporting high pointed arches; the polygonal apse is lit with small round openings and large double-arched windows, as well as the ogival windows in the naves which shed light into the almost undivided internal space.
On the right-hand side of the church are the first and second cloisters. Near the first is the Pazzi Chapel, the famous masterpiece by Brunelleschi commissioned Andrea de' Pazzi in 1429. This building resembles the Old Sacristy of San Lorenzo, with an external portico of stone Corinthian columns, and with two internal spaces, one small and the other larger, roofed with a ribbed umbrella dome, flanked by two barrel vaults. Around the whole perimeter is a bench and pilasters supporting the structure designed in stone.

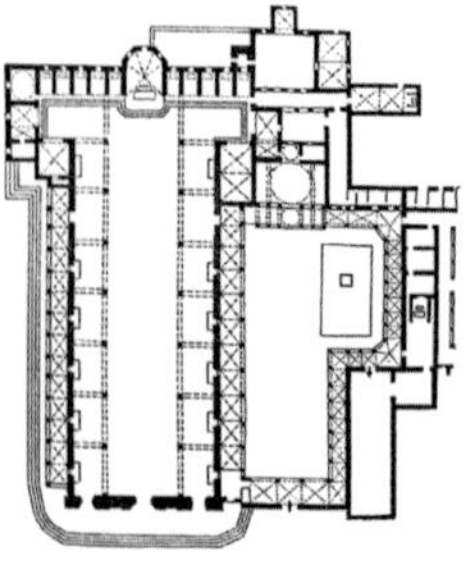

architects
Arnolfo di Cambio, Filippo Brunelleschi, Francesco da Sangallo, Niccolò Matas

type
church

construction
Church: 1294-1443 (façade) 1853-1863
Bell tower: 1842-1847
Pazzi Chapel: 1430-1470 circa

24. Central National Library

Piazza dei Cavalleggeri 1
50122, Florence

Mon - Fri / 8.15 am - 7 pm
Sat / 8.15 am - 1.30 pm
Sun / closed

+39 055 249191

www.bncf.firenze.sbn.it

23 > Zecca Vecchia Nazionale
C3 > Magliabechi

Originally located in the Uffizi palace, the current library building is the result of a national public competition launched in 1902. The construction began in 1911, the corner gallery was built in 1929, and the building was completed in 1935. The structure has changed considerably in comparison to the original plans. In 1962, a large extension was added in Via Magliabechi, and restoration work was carried out in 1974 and 1990.
Together with the main entrance facing the Arno, recalling the traditional Florentine loggia, an unusual feature is the corner gallery with its domed roof. The exterior is built in sandstone, concrete and majolica, while the internal materials are pietra serena, marble and granite, with ornamental elements and refined wooden and steel furnishings on all three floors. Access is through the raised portico into the vestibule, atrium, and the large centre room with overhead skylights. This leads into the reading room, catalogue room, and the semi-circular area with the various departments and storerooms containing 40 km of shelving that continue as far as the Chiostro di Santa Croce. The basement space is used for storage and workshops, while two serena stone staircases in the atrium lead to the first floor that houses the study rooms and spaces for bibliographic exhibitions.

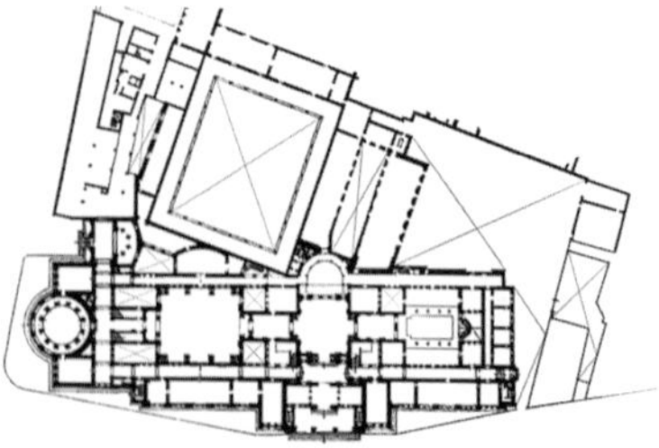

architects
Cesare Bazzani / Vincenzo Mazzei (extension in Via Magliabechi)

type
library

construction
1911-1935
1962 (extension in Via Magliabechi)

25. Ponte alle Grazie

Ponte alle Grazie
50125, Florence

open to the public

23/D > Demidoff
C3 > Mozzi
C3/C1 > Diaz

Originally built in 1237, the bridge was first called Ponte Rubaconte, after the Podestà of Florence, Rubaconte da Mandello. It was given its current name because of a small chapel built on the bridge in the 14th century, dedicated to Santa Maria delle Grazie. During the 19th century, the bridge underwent considerable changes, and was then destroyed in August 1944 by the German army during their retreat. A competition for bridge reconstruction was announced the following year, won by architects Edoardo Detti, Riccardo Gizdulich, Giovanni Michelucci, Danilo Santi, and the engineer, Piero Melucci. The structure was based on massive amounts of reinforced concrete, softened with facings in sandstone and plaster finish, both traditional Florentine materials. The structure consists of a reinforced concrete Gerber girder with five arches of different lengths. The six ribbings with a lower curved profile are connected underneath by a continuous bottom flange of varying thickness, and above, by the carriageway bed and the crossbeams that support the raised pavements. The parapet is composed of alternating solid and void sections that create an interesting rhythm across the length of the bridge.

© Neri Casamonti

architects
Giovanni Michelucci, Edoardo Detti, Riccardo Gizdulich, Danilo Santi, Piero Melucci

type
bridge

construction
1955-1957

26. Museo Galileo

Piazza dei Giudici 1
50122, Florence

January - December
Mon - Sun / 9.30 am - 6 pm
Tue / 9.30 am - 1 pm

+39 055 265311
info@museogalileo.it
www.museogalileo.it

C1/C3 > Diaz

Following complex restauration and exhibition staging work, the Museo Galileo was reopened in June 2010 at Palazzo Castellani, which previously housed the History of Science Museum. The building has six floors, and as well as the Museo Galileo, it houses the History of Science Institute, a library, offices, congress rooms, and spaces for temporary exhibitions. The intervention involved the redesigning of the entire exhibition system aimed at maximising the layout of the building as well as the collections on show to give the public a unified perception during museum visits.
The exhibition route follows a circular path through the eighteen rooms on the first and second floors with special display cases containing the 1,300 instruments belonging to the de' Medici and Lorraine collections. The itinerary is diversified with a wide variety of materials, colours and partitions, to highlight specially themed backgrounds for the most important instruments and collections. These include the Globe Room, arranged around Santucci's great armillary sphere, and the Galileo Rooms that lead to the extraordinary collection of glass instruments from the Accademia del Cimento.

© Natalini Architetti

architects
Natalini Architetti, Guicciardini & Magni Architetti Studio Associato

type
museum

construction
2007-2010

27. Loggia del Grano and ex Capitol Renovation

Via dei Castellani 6
50122, Florence

external viewing only

C1/C3 > Galleria degli Uffizi

This building forms the corner of an urban block opposite the exit from the Uffizi Museum, and is partly linked with the 19th century construction above the Loggia del Grano designed by Parigi.
The original layout formed the Teatro delle Logge, created in 1868 by the architect, Andrea Scala. It was transformed several times and in 1935, it had a seating capacity of 1,200.
In 1953, architect Nello Baroni was commissioned to rebuild the complex including a new stage structure, a staircase/elevator, and a new design for the area above the loggia.
The Capitol Cinema-theatre was opened in 1957, and later modified by Gamberini. It was in constant use for thirty years, then closed and abandoned.
At the end of the 1990s, Natalini Architetti and S.IN.Ter redeveloped the building, redesigning the internal function; the space was used for cultural, tourism and recreational activities, (tourist market, bar restaurant, office spaces). As well as the internal layout, the façade on Via dei Castellani was changed to re-introduce the string course bands of the previous building, aligning them with the adjacent Loggia del Grano, but creating rows of narrow regular windows.

© Mario Ciampi

architects
Natalini Architetti

type
multi-purpose building

construction
1998-2004

28. Palazzo Vecchio - Uffizi Museum

Palazzo Vecchio:
Piazza della Signoria
Uffizi Museum:
Piazzale degli Uffizi 6
50122, Florence

Palazzo Vecchio:
open to the public
+39 055 2768325
www.museicivicifiorentini.
comune.fi.it/palazzovecchio

Uffizi Museum:
January - December
Tue - Sun / 8.15 am - 6.50 pm
+39 055 23885
ga-uff@beniculturali.it
www.uffizi.it

C1/C3 > Galleria degli Uffizi
C2 > Condotta
C3/D >Ponte Vecchio

Construction of the Palazzo dei Priori began in 1299; it later became the headquarters of the Signoria and today belongs to the Comune di Firenze; it was renamed Palazzo Vecchio in 1565, when Duke Cosimo I de' Medici moved his court to Palazzo Pitti. Traditionally attributed to Arnolfo di Cambio, the building was initially rectangular and built on an area once occupied by an ancient Roman theatre. Its imposing stone ashlar façade rises above the piazza, featuring gothic-styled double-arched windows and castellated crown on the protruding gallery over jutting brackets. The high tower, built in 1310, using the stone from the pre-existent Foraboschi tower, called "della Vacca", was misaligned in the southern direction. Supervised by artists like Michelozzo, Vasari, Ammannati and Buontalenti, and commissioned by clients like Cosimo I, over the centuries, the building underwent massive extensions and transformations in the eastern direction expanding the building to four times its original size.
Adjacent to the palace and overlooking the Arno is the Uffizi gallery complex. It was built by Cosimo I to unite the 13 Judiciary Bodies of the city, and it was only after 1581, that the Uffizi was used for other purposes, mainly as a museum. The complex was designed by Vasari following the demolition of about 300 dwellings, freeing the space for a U-shaped building with an open central square leading to the piazza della Signoria. It is composed of two parallel wings, with a lengthwise modular layout, connected by a crosswise structure, built on the flood plain of the Arno and overlooking the river with a wide Serlian window. The long stone and white rendered façades are composed of a tripartite trabeated portico, internally covered with barrel-vaulted ceilings, a fascia with rectangular openings, a main floor with gabled windows and topped with a large loggia enclosed with tall windows.

architects
Palazzo Vecchio: Arnolfo di Cambio, Michelozzo, Giorgio Vasari, Bartolomeo Ammannati, Bernardo Buontalenti
Uffizi Museum: Giorgio Vasari, Alfonso Parigi, Bernardo Buontalenti

type
museum, offices

construction
Palazzo Vecchio: 1299-1596
1809-1989 (renovation)
Uffizi Museum: 1560-1580

29. Scala di Ponente, New Uffizi Extension

Piazzale degli Uffizi 6
50122, Florence

January - December
Tue - Sun / 8.15 am - 6.50 pm

Uffizi Museum:
+39 055 23885
ga-uff@beniculturali.it
www.uffizi.it

C1/C3 > Galleria degli Uffizi

The New Uffizi project involves doubling the current exhibition capacity of the museum with restoration and renovation work and functional upgrading of the first-floor rooms of the Gallery. The project is still underway, but certain elements, such as the Scala di Ponente designed by Natalini Architetti, have been completed.
The staircase is located in a small courtyard close to the Loggia dei Lanzi and resembles a stone tower with voids through which the staircase can be seen. The ramps are clad with burnished bronze wrapped around the base of the stairs to form a parapet. The handrail is underlined with a light strip that continues for the entire height of the staircase. Roofing with skylights and a series of windows provide light and shelter inside the courtyard transforming it into a new internal space where modern design blends with historic architecture.
The Scala di Levante, also designed by Natalini Architetti, will be built in a position symmetrical to the Scala di Ponente, in the area that sits between the remains of the Church of San Pier Scheraggio and the Vasari staircase.

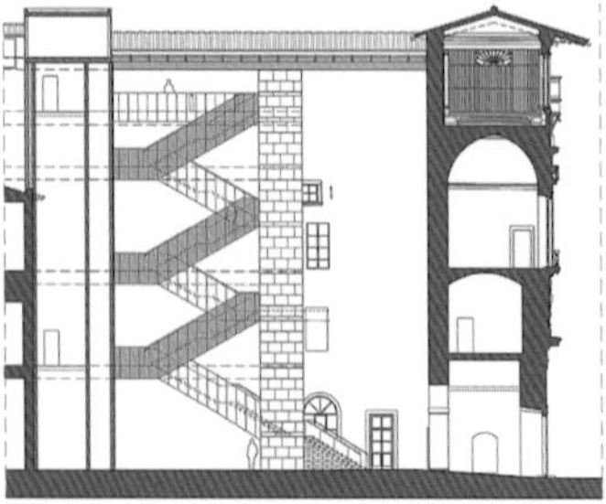

architects
Natalini Architetti

type
museum

construction
2003-2011

30. Sale dei Primitivi

Piazzale degli Uffizi 6
50122, Florence

January - December
Tue - Sun / 8.15 am - 6.50 pm

Uffizi Museum:
+39 055 23885
ga-uff@beniculturali.it
www.uffizi.it

C1/C3 > Galleria degli Uffizi

The so-called "Sale dei Primitivi" are 6 rooms (numbers 2 to 7) in the Uffizi Museum complex designed in the 1950s. They are located in the eastern wing in what was formerly the Medici theatre, commissioned by Francesco I, and designed by Buontalenti.
The layout features different solutions for lighting, roof skylights and communicating openings between exhibition spaces, to best display the works by artists such as Cimabue, Giotto and Pollaiolo. The main architectural elements include wooden trusses to recall Medieval churches; the moving of doorways to the corners to maximise wall space, sometimes painted bright colours to provide contrast for the art works, and vertical slots in walls to create visual connections between the different rooms and facilitate art work transport. Modulated light using skylights, a large horizontal window along the base of the ceiling trusses, and traditional type windows, provide extra light.
As part of the New Uffizi project, the lighting and air conditioning installations were upgraded between 2014 and 2015. At the same time, elegant restructuration and scientific reorganisation work was carried out, supervised by Antonio Natali and Daniela Parenti.

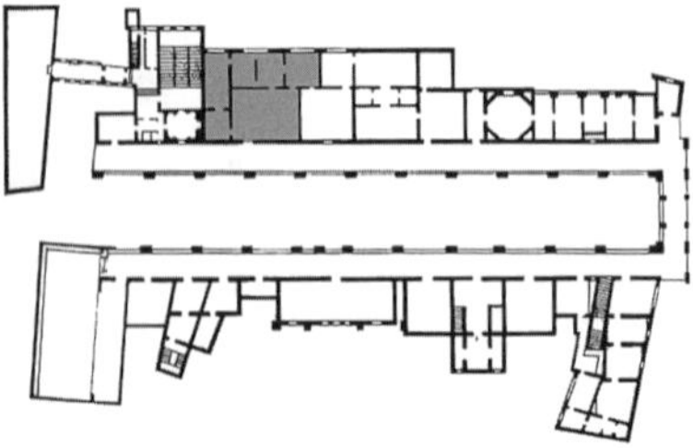

architects
Ignazio Gardella, Giovanni Michelucci, Carlo Scarpa, Guido Morozzi

type
museum

construction
1953-1957
2014-2015 (renovation)

31. Ponte Vecchio - Vasari Corridor - Palazzo Pitti

Ponte Vecchio:
Ponte Vecchio
Vasari Corridor:
from Piazza della Signoria to Piazza de' Pitti
Palazzo Pitti:
Piazza de' Pitti 1
50125, Florence

Ponte Vecchio:
external viewing only

Vasari Corridor:
group visits on reservation

Palazzo Pitti:
January - December
Tue - Sun / 8.15 am - 6.50 pm
Mon / closed

C3/D > Bardi, Ponte Vecchio
11 > Piazza San Felice

Ponte Vecchio, the oldest in Florence, and the only bridge to survive German mines in 1944, crosses the Arno at its narrowest point. Ever since Etruscan times, there had always been a wooden bridge at this point, repeatedly destroyed by fires and floods. After the flood in 1333, a three-span bridge was rebuilt in stone, with about 40 small shops lining the pavements, then extended to project over the river in later years. Only the centre part was left free, where three arches permitted views over the Arno. Initially these were butchers' shops, but following the construction of the Vasari corridor that crossed the entire length of the bridge above the shops, they were then converted to goldsmiths' boutiques. The Corridor, a suspended covered road 760 metres long, connected Palazzo Vecchio with Palazzo Pitti, and was built in 1565 (when Palazzo Pitti became the Ducal residence. Commissioned by Cosimo I, Vasari designed the corridor which was completed in only eight months. Converted to an exhibition space in 1866, small round windows in the corridor overlook the city, while larger rectangular windows provide views of the Arno. In 1588-89, the corridor was extended from the Buontalenti Grotto in the Giardino di Boboli to the interior of Palazzo Pitti. This large palace has magnificent gardens at the rear while the front façade overlooks Piazza Pitti. The powerful stone façade decreases in height on each side, and has regular rows of windows with rounded arched frames. The initial building, now the central structure, replaced the previous Pitti residence, probably designed by Brunelleschi. It was later extended by Ammannati, who created the courtyard. In the 17th century, Giulio Parigi carried out further extensions by adding two wings aligned symmetrically with the palace, followed by two semi-circular constructions at the sides, completed in 1840.

architects
Ponte Vecchio: Taddeo Gaddi, Neri di Fioravante, Fra Domenico da Campi
Vasari Corridor: Giorgio Vasari
Palazzo Pitti: Filippo Brunelleschi, Luca Fancelli, Bartolomeo Ammannati, Alfonso Parigi, Giulio Parigi, Giuseppe Ruggieri, Pasquale Poccianti

type
museum, retail

construction
Ponte Vecchio: 1339-1345
Vasari Corridor: 1565-1589
Palazzo Pitti: 1457-1840

32. Ponte Vecchio area reconstruction

Via Por Santa Maria, Via Guicciardini, the first section of Via de' Bardi and Borgo San Jacopo, including the buildings overlooking the Arno

external viewing only

C3/D > Bardi, Ponte Vecchio

This project refers to post-war reconstruction made necessary when German mines destroyed five of Florence's bridges on August 4th, 1944, leaving only the Ponte Vecchio and surrounding area intact. A competition for the reconstruction of the damaged areas was decided on December 11, 1945, following heated cultural debates between those who wanted redevelopment in a modern style, and those who felt the area should be rebuilt "as it was, where it was".
The reconstruction involved Via Por Santa Maria, Via Guicciardini, the first section of Via de' Bardi and Borgo San Jacopo, including the buildings overlooking the Arno.
The discussions led to a solution of compromise, mainly based on a form of camouflage: The façades are modern but based on traditional proportions, buildings are irregular heights with corbelled cornices projecting over the river bank and façades are finished in plaster render alongside stone-clad portions. Giovanni Michelucci, who sustained the idea of non-conservationist reconstruction, did not take part in the competition, but in 1954, he designed the Ina building for residential apartments and retail stores on the corner of Via Guicciardini and via dello Sprone. For its time, this building represents one of the main architectural examples of strong Medieval style expressed with a modern interpretation.

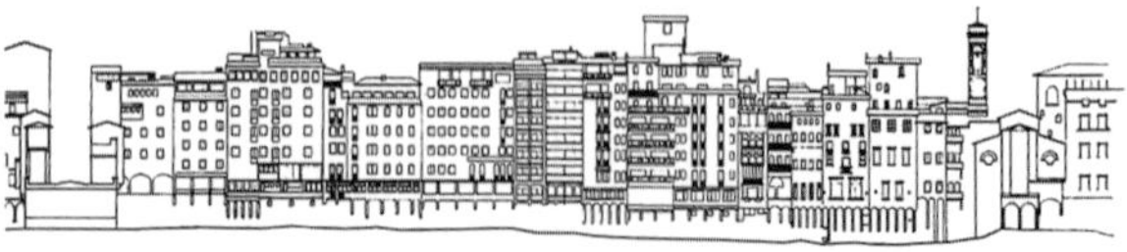

architects
Lando Bartoli, Edoardo Detti, Italo Gamberini, Giovanni Michelucci, Leonardo Ricci, Leonardo Savioli, Francesco Tiezzi, Uffici Tecnici Comunali

type
residential, retail

construction
1945-1958

33. Church of Santo Spirito

Piazza Santo Spirito 30
50125, Florence

Mon - Sun / 10 am - 12.30 am, 4 pm - 6 pm
Wed / closed

www.basilicasantospirito.it/

C3/D > Santo Spirito
11 > Piazza San Felice

The Augustinian Church of Santo Spirito, whose 18th century plaster-rendered façade, with its centre oculus and triple entrances, built on the site of a pre-existent 13th century church, is now an iconic monument on the southern side of the Arno. The present building was designed by Brunelleschi and building began in 1444. Originally planned to face towards the Arno, after Brunelleschi's death in 1446, it was completed by Antonio Manetti, Giovanni da Gaiole and Salvi d'Andrea who made several changes to the initial design.
The interior recalls many characteristics of San Lorenzo, but in a more complex and dynamic design: the stone structural framework with monolithic columns and Corinthian capitals divide the Latin Cross layout into three naves, and the crossing is roofed by a dome. Around the perimeter are 40 semicircular apse chapels whose rear walls were designed to form the external walls of the church. The left nave leads into a vestibule and sacristy designed by Giuliano da Sangallo, and on the left side of the façade are the first cloister by Alfonso and Giulio Parigi, the new refectory and the Santo Spirito Cenacle. These are followed by the second cloister by Ammannati (1564-69) and the Corsini Chapel. The bell tower erected in 1503 by Baccio d'Agnolo, has two rows of arched windows and an elegant belfry topped with a pyramid-shaped pinnacle.

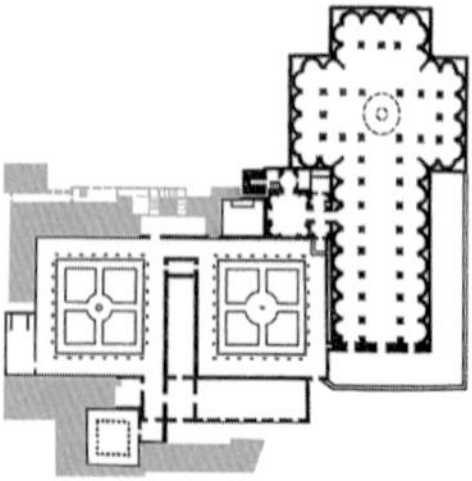

architects
Filippo Brunelleschi, Antonio Manetti, Giovanni da Gaiole, Salvi d'Andrea

type
church

construction
Church: 1444-1487
Bell tower: 1503-1541

34. Piedibus Project

Via della Chiesa
50125, Florence

open to the public

11 > Campuccio
11/13/36/37 >
Firenze Piazza Tasso
Per Fi

This redevelopment project is based on a strategic intervention designed for pedestrian safety between school and home in the Oltrarno district: Pedibus is a sustainable concept, a safe, clean and socially educational system and group project which has not only redeveloped this section of an urban street, but has transformed it into a meeting place.
This is the first intervention in a plan composed of several micro-projects: it is a new urban space near the Torrigiani school and the Albergo Popolare, where for a section of about 40 metres, the vehicle carriageway has been narrowed and the pedestrian pavement has been widened to create diverse areas using different paving stone surfaces. A platform 4 metres wide in local sandstone, raised a little above street level, is constructed in front of the access to the school entrance. Two gently sloping ramps are protected by a low stone wall and the walkway has recessed led steplights. The zone is equipped with solid stone seating and two smooth stone "chalkboards" inserted into the pavement for children to draw with coloured chalks. On the opposite side of the street, connected by a raised pedestrian crossing that acts as a speed-break, a pedestrian zone has been created in front of the Albergo Popolare.

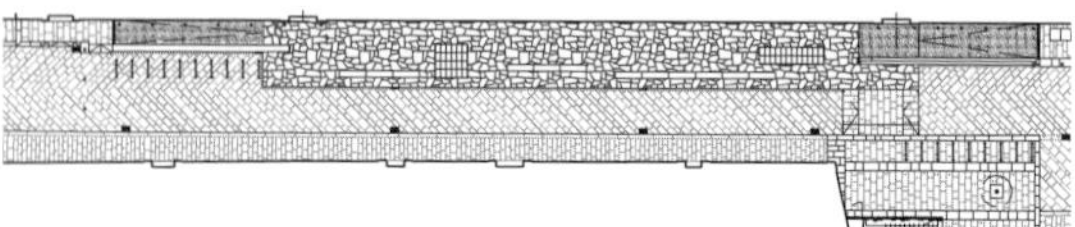

architects
studiostudio
architettiurbanisti

type
public space

construction
2006-2009

35. Casa della Finestra

Piazza Torquato Tasso 1
50124 Florence

external viewing only

13/36/37 > Firenze Piazza Tasso Per Fi

This building is the result of restructuration work on the ancient complex of the Scuole Leopoldine, begun in the late nineties. The structure dates back to 1102 when it was a Camaldolese convent, later a leper hospital in 1523, a "hospice for beggars" in 1622, and under the Grand Duke Peter Leopold, it became the headquarters of the "Free school for poor spinsters of the Santo Spirito neighbourhood". After a fire in 1978, the former convent fell into a state of bad disrepair.
The intervention was aimed at creating public housing for needy families, with certain multifunctional spaces open to the public.
The façade profile protrudes slightly in relation to the street line, so that the front is detached from the structure of the bastion set further back. The wedge-shaped wall is faced in sandstone, and despite the difference in slab sizes and colour shades, it appears like a monolithic slab interrupted only in the upper left-hand corner by a large cross-framed opening.
Climbing upwards, the internal staircase incorporates small spaces to pause and view the city panorama; it terminates with a large loggia space, designed for exhibitions, congresses and public events.

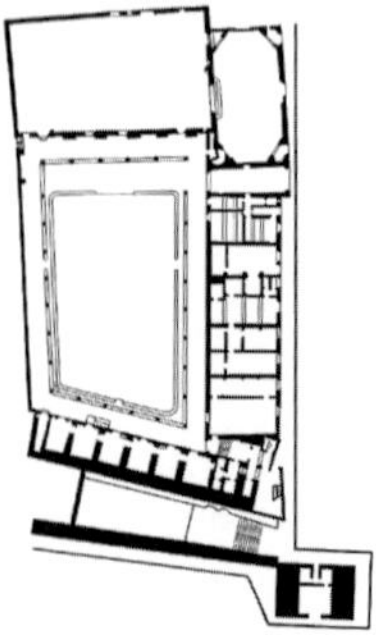

© Neri Casamonti

architects
Zermani e Associati

type
multi-purpose building

construction
1998-2005

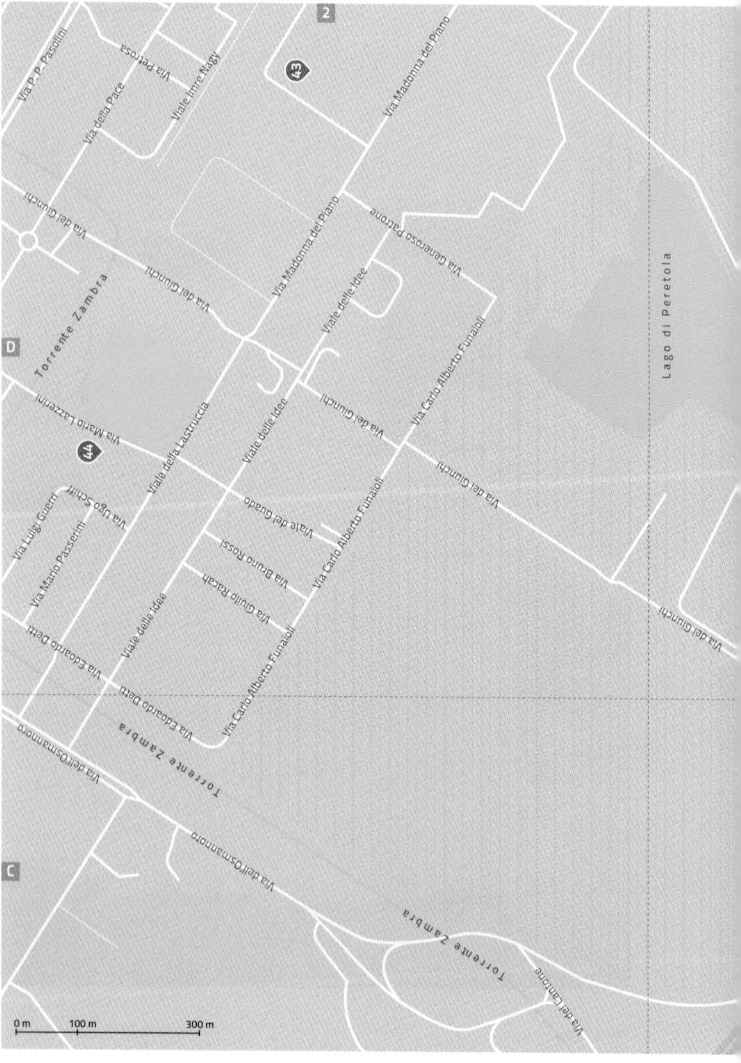
2
D
C
Via P. P. Pasolini
Via Petrosa
Viale Imre Nagy
Via della Pace
Via Madonna del Piano
Via dei Giunchi
Torrente Zambra
Via Generoso Patrone
Viale delle Idee
Via Carlo Alberto Funaioli
Lago di Peretola
Via Mario Lazzerini
Viale della Lastruccia
Via Ugo Schiff
Via Luigi Guerri
Via Mario Passerini
Viale del Guado
Via Bruno Rossi
Via Giulio Racah
Via Edoardo Detti
Via dell'Osmannoro
Via del Cantone
0 m
100 m
300 m

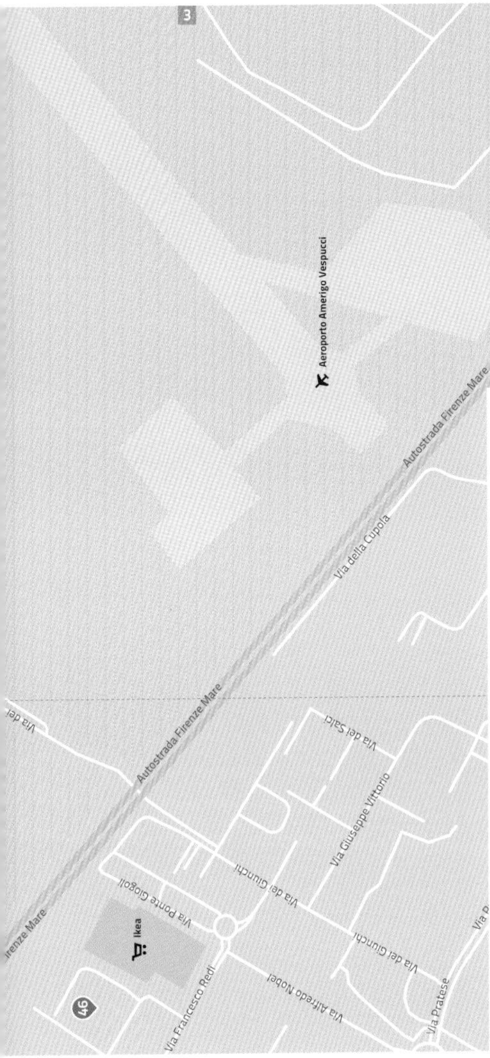

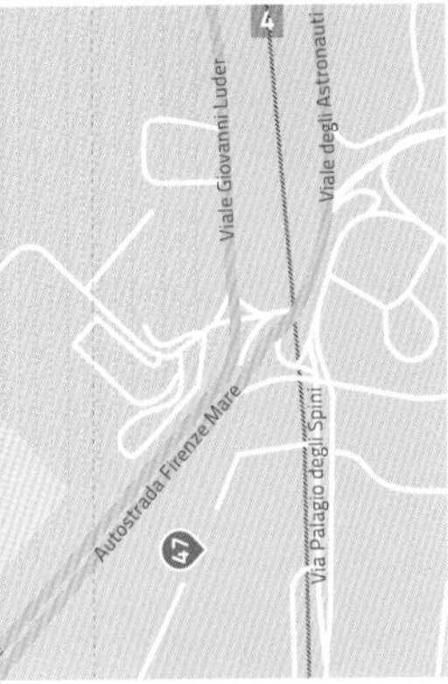

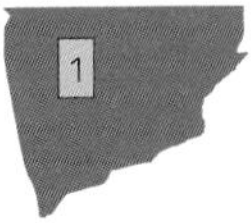

Florence North-West

36. Spadolini Pavilion
37. Fondiaria Insurance Building
38. Santa Maria Novella Station Thermal Plant and Controls
39. Statuto Railway Station
40. Careggi Hospital Entrance
41. Meyer Children's Hospital Complex
42. La Fonte Sports Gym
43. Florence University Incubator
44. Villa Val di Rose University Student Residence
45. Church of San Giovanni Battista, called "Chiesa dell'Autostrada"
46. Restoration - BP Studio
47. Meeting Point Centre
48. Le Navi Housing

Florence North-West

49. Indiano Bridge Viaduct
50. Isolotto Quarter
51. Scandicci Civic Centre
52. Military Aviation Institute
53. Opera Theatre
54. Entrance Piazza to the ex Leopolda Station
55. Ex Singer Building
56. San Jacopino Condominium
57. Evergreen University Student Residence
58. Ex Tobacco Plant and Puccini Theatre
59. Novoli Quarter
60. Florence Law Courts
61. Cassa di Risparmio di Firenze Building
62. Firenze Nova Residential Complex

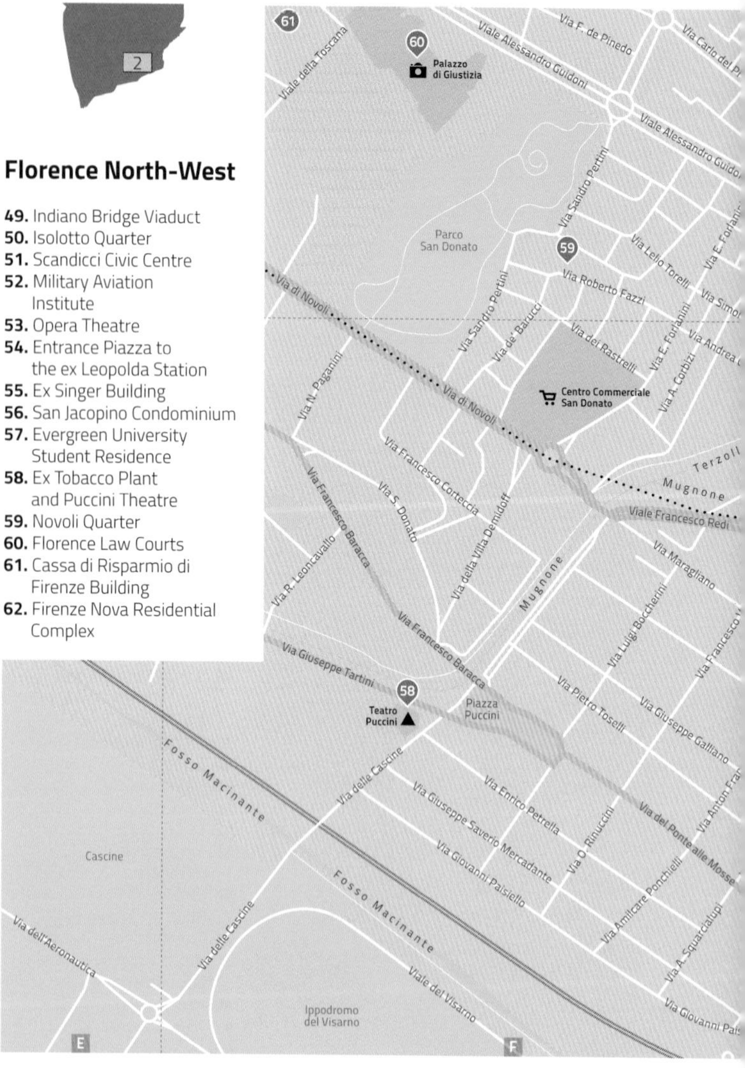

0 m
100 m
300 m
Via Vittorio Emanuele II
Via Taddeo Alderotti
Via Michele Mercati
Via Celso
Via di Rifredi
Navigatore
Via Benedetto Dei
Terzolle
Via Giovan Filippo Mariti
Via del Terzolle
Via Carlo Pisacane
Via Vittorio Emanuele II
Via G. D. Romagnosi
Viale Corsica
Via P. Della Valle
Via Filippo Corridoni
Terzolle
Antonio Pigafetta
Via Riguccio Galluzzi
Piazza Leopoldo
Via Ponte di Mezzo
Via Giovan Filippo Mariti
Via Giovanni dei Marignolli
Via dell'Arcovata
Via Pompeo Neri
Viale Corsica
Via Odorico da Pordenone
Via Piero Cironi
Via Enrico Mayer
Via Circondaria
Via del Romito
Via Circondaria
Via Gaetano Milanesi
Via Scipio Sighele
Viale Corsica
Viale Francesco Redi
Via Luigi Gordigliani
Via del Romito
Via Maragliano
Via Vincenzo Bellini
Viale F. Fontana
Viale Francesco Redi
Viale dei Cadorna
Viale F. Pachini
Via Claudio Monteverdi
Via G. T. Tozzetti
Via Maragliano
Mugnone
Via del Romito
Via S. Jacopino
Viale Francesco Redi
Via Giuseppe Galliano
Via Cosseria
Via Guido Spadolini
Via Gaspare Luigi Spontini
Via Pietro Toselli
Via D. Cimarosa
Via Cassia
del Ponte alle Mosse
Viale Filippo Strozzi
Via Benedetto Marcello
Porpora
Via Giovanni Paisiello
Fortezza da Basso
4
5
G
56
57
38

36. Spadolini Pavilion

Viale Filippo Strozzi 1
50129, Florence

open to the public only during specific events

+39 055 49721
info@firenzefiera.it
www.firenzefiera.it

6/11/14/17 >
Stazione Arrivi
1/4/6/11/14/17/ 23/52/54/82 >
Indipendenza

La Fortezza da Basso was comissioned by Alessandro de' Medici and built by Pier Francesco da Viterbo and Antonio da Sangallo il Giovane between 1534 and 1537. In later centuries, it was used as an arsenal and foundry, a storage deposit for the Grand Dukes of Tuscany, and a reformatory, after which it became military property until it was assigned to its present role as exhibition space for fairs and congresses.
The walls of the fortress enclose a space of about 9 hectares, containing several buildings constructed over the centuries. The pavilion designed by Spadolini remains below the height of the fortress walls and creates a dialogue using bronze anodised aluminium, a contemporary material, able to convey a sense of strength and force with its continuous profile. The entire structure is built of steel, using a single type of pillar and two kinds of beams. The external stairs are made of prefabricated concrete elements with green and white river pebble inserts. The pavilion covers a surface of 27,000 square metres with separate entrances to the two floors, so that both spaces can be used simultaneously. Four large symmetrical ramps run up the long side of the structure leading to the roof-terrace.

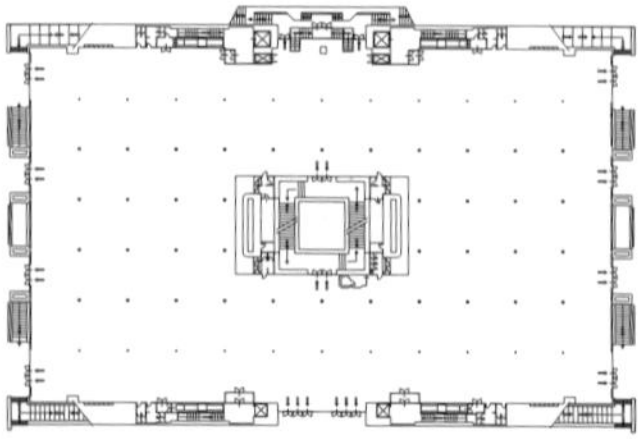

architects
Pierluigi Spadolini

tipologia
exhibition space

construction
1974-1976

37. Fondiaria Insurance Building

Viale Spartaco Lavagnini 40-42-44-46
50129, Florence

4/8/20 > Lavagnini Leone X

As with his other Florentine projects of the same period, Italo Gamberini placed this building in a well-consolidated urban fabric – in this case, the wide streets designed by Giuseppe Poggi in the late 19th century, seeking affinity with the context but without necessarily wanting to imitate the style.
The windows create a regular rhythm on the façade, similar to the surrounding 19th century buildings, but the eaves provide a three-dimensional play of shadow that gives the façade a strongly contemporary appearance. Other elements that recall traditional Florentine architecture can be seen in Gamberini's project, like the imposing cornice around the top of the façade, the recessed ground floor that acts as the base of the building, and the Silipol slab facing in a sandstone colour. The functional layout features a metal staircase, designed with great attention to detail.

architects
Italo Gamberini, Loris Macci

type
offices

construction
1962-1965

38. Santa Maria Novella Station Thermal Plant and Controls

Via delle Ghiacciaie 2
50144, Florence

external viewing only

This architecture, rich in Futurist-Constructivist-Expressionist references, makes a formal statement concerning the functions performed within the building. Although it was constructed as an organic complex, it is composed of two individual buildings connected by a semi-circular element that acts as a link. The first block houses the thermal plant which heats the interior of the station. It is composed of a parallelepiped topped by four chimney stacks, one for each of the four boilers in the building. They can be accessed by a helical stairway and walkway. The second block houses the controls cabin for track changes and railway signals; pivoted in relation to the first building, it is composed of parallelepiped block with rounded ends, and a large projecting glazed window section overlooks the rail tracks along the entire length of the upper part of the block.
The reinforced concrete used in structural framing permits free communication between the different blocks and levels to form a well-structured layout, placing the urban road system on the same level as the railway tracks. Externally, the building is clad with exposed brick and plaster render painted dark red. Trims and cornices are in light travertine stone, while the brass window frames recall the windows of the main railway station nearby.

23 > Viale Fratelli Rosselli 66

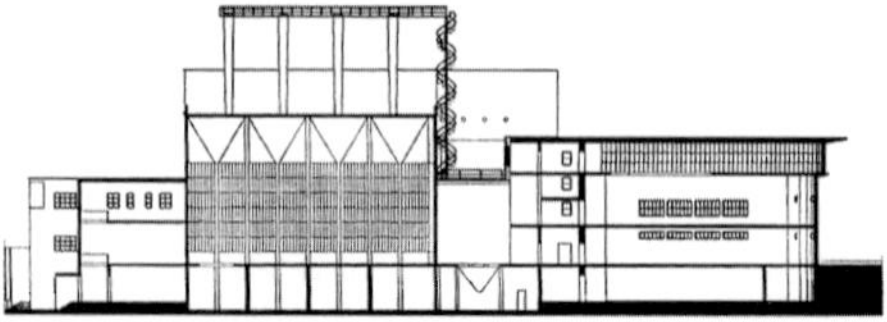

architects
Angiolo Mazzoni

type
offices

construction
1927-1934

39. Statuto Railway Station

Piazza Ludovico Antonio Muratori
50134, Florence

open to the public

2/4/8/20/28 > Statuto

In 1985, the State Railways Special Unit (II) decided to redesign the Firenze Statuto Railway Station, initially destined for regional train transit only, but also planned for later use as a stop for Rome-Milan high speed trains (later re-routed to Firenze Rifredi). As a result, the project was modified according to new necessities. The construction along the railway track had to be extended; the pavement length was increased to 250 metres, and the overhanging shelters and structure façade were extended to a length of 140 metres. However, the station's initial scenographic concept was maintained to represent a new "gateway" to the city. The structure presents a series of historical references: the Vierendeel trusses recall steel railway bridges, and the original structure is reminiscent of Ammannati's stone river bridges. Another reference is the window by Buontalenti, which Toraldo di Francia decided to incorporate in the project. It sits on the steel structure like a symbolic bridge between exterior and interior, city and suburban areas. The station was opened in 1988.

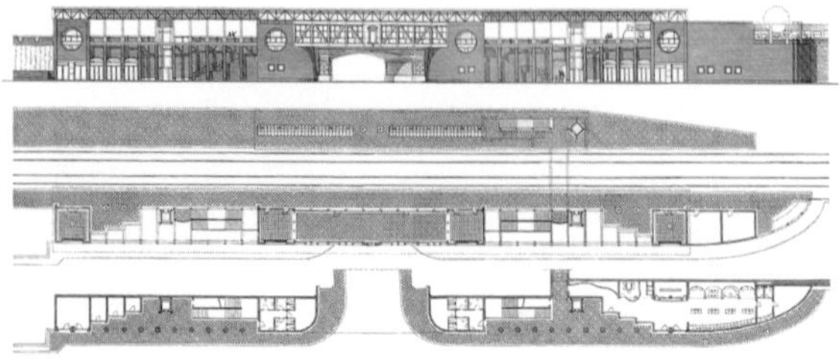

architects
Cristiano Toraldo di Francia

type
railway station

construction
1985-1988

40. Careggi Hospital Entrance

Largo Brambilla 3
50134, Florence

open to the public

+39 055 794111
aouc@aou-careggi.toscana.it
www.aou-careggi.toscana.it

14/40/43 > Brambilla

The multifunctional and management centre of the new Careggi Hospital entrance performs a double role as an interface with the city and the access to the entire hospital campus.

This project was aimed at overcoming the enclosed, somewhat hostile aspect of the hospital entrance by creating a new passageway and meeting area in the form of a covered piazza. It continues the traditional Florentine style with loggias, ample seating, and a large pool. The pedestrian piazza, paved with serena stone is covered by a 15 metre-high portico supported by tall steel columns. The 2,500 square metre roof is composed of a skylight grid that provides overhead lighting; the roofing covers all or part of the four buildings of the complex incorporating all into a single unit. The hall forms the central space with a full-height glazed ceiling: a large luminous area that can cope with a daily flow of twenty thousand members of the public per day. The management centre is also equipped with services for the public, information structures, administration and university services and retail stores. The complex also houses a three-storey car park for 429 vehicles.

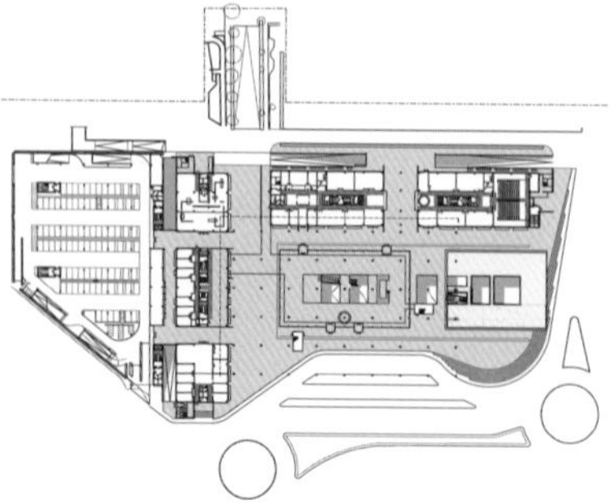

architects
CSPE, Elio Di Franco, Ipostudio

type
service

construction
1999-2011

41. Meyer Children's Hospital Complex

Viale Gaetano Pieraccini 24
50139, Florence

open to the public

+39 055 56621

www.meyer.it

14/43/R > Pieraccini 07

The new Meyer Children's Hospital is the combination of the psycho-sensorial analysis of architectural space and respect for the surrounding environment: a historic park, an early 20th century villa, and a hill of outstanding natural beauty. Cutting edge technology, careful choice of materials, and environmental sustainability are integrated to establish reciprocal synergy. Although the three pavilions of the original Villa Ognissanti were not suitable for a modern hospital complex, the villa was conserved as a support structure, while the main care facilities are concentrated in the new building. The shape of the Careggi hill influenced the evolution of the sunken solution adopted for the project. Two floors are built below ground and only the third is completely above ground. Seen from above, the new pavilion harmonises with the surrounding landscape, following the natural curves of the terrain, with large planted terraces, and a green roof garden.
Stress factors associated with hospitalisation were studied according to therapeutic architectural concepts borrowed from evidence-based design; this inspired the decision to restore the entrance building, creating a bioclimatic space flooded with light, and taking advantage of the historic arbour that winds through the park, providing a psychologically relaxing route leading to the hospital entrance.

© CSPE

architects
CSPE

type
hospital

construction
2000-2009

42. La Fonte Sports Gym

Via Arrigo Boito 5
50019, Sesto Fiorentino

open to the public

2/28/86 > Sesto Fiorentino Gramsci 02

The building is based on a very simple stereometric form composed of two rectangular elements of different heights that reflect their principal functions: the taller flared building houses the sports area, and forms the main core of the complex; the smaller building, almost seems like a fragment that has grown out of the main structure, attached to one corner; it contains the changing rooms and technical equipment services.
While the changing room building, faced in Tivoli travertine slabs, seems to define a walled horizon, the sports building represents the idea of a body in motion, expanding outwards from inside the building until it appears on the external surface. The effect is one of muscular fibre, as seen in Leonardo's anatomy drawings, embodied in the changing effects of the copper facing. The facing expands, generating a body that broadens as it rises, almost organic in nature. This effect is emphasised by the materials: rows of undulating copper strips assembled without nails or other fixing methods, permitting the metal to expand and retract according to the temperature and the seasons.

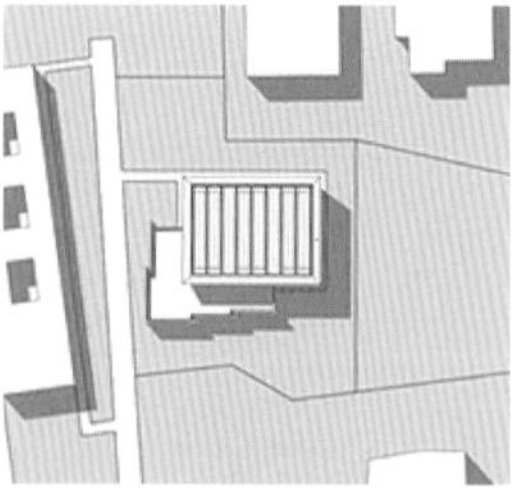

© Fabio Capanni

architects
Fabio Capanni

type
sports centre

construction
1997-2006

43. Florence University Incubator

Via Madonna del Piano 5
50019, Sesto Fiorentino

January - December
Mon - Fri / 7.30 am - 7 pm

+39 055 4574600
iuf@csvari.unifi.it
www.bio.unifi.it

59/66 > Madonna del Piano

This complex, inaugurated in 2010, houses the Florence University Incubator that promotes and supports the birth and early development stages of university start-ups and spin-offs based on ideas with high innovation levels and closely linked with university research.
The building is composed of four blocks arranged symmetrically from north to south, aligned with the detailed town planning rules that govern the Polo Scientifico in Sesto. The plan specified the construction of a number of identical square urban blocks, closed on all sides, but in this case, Fabrizio Rossi Prodi proposed a large solid structure, but providing access between the blocks with views into the interior. Like the structure, the outer shell, distribution and logics, the internal mechanisms were divided and opened up to form counterbalanced elements.
The main building elements are developed along the same architectural theme that differentiates the shell from the internal structure and that reveals the interrupted section of the building wall, both at the front and along the street, repeating the theme of a semi-open urban block with its architectural style.

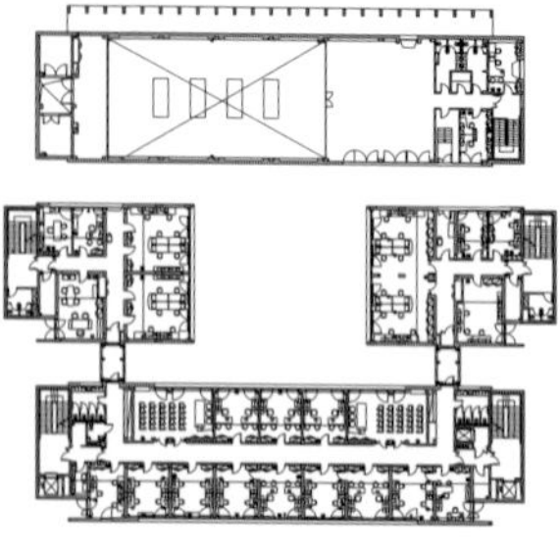

architects
Fabrizio Rossi Prodi

type
university

construction
2002-2010

44. Villa Val di Rose University Student Residence

Via Lazzerini 202
50019, Sesto Fiorentino

57/66 > Neruda

This project is composed of two interventions: the renovation and conservation of the so-called "Villa Val di Rose", and, in an area adjacent to the villa, the construction of a new complex, composed of two buildings as a residence for approximately a hundred students. The two new, long rectangular buildings converge towards each other and are connected by two glazed covered walkways. The first building, aligned with the street, houses all student services, while the second building to the rear, contains the student residence.
The services block is composed of a single floor and is partially enclosed by a higher inverted L-shaped wall entirely clad in travertine slab, interrupted by a few long slim windows. The reduced height is in proportion with the street and respects the surrounding and adjacent buildings.
In strong contrast with the white surface of the first building, the residential block is clad in brick, and is punctuated by regular rows of windows and several projecting steel and glass balconies. The building has three floors with two large staircases and is arranged in three blocks visible from the front façade. The two outer sections are composed of integrated apartments composed of 6 bedrooms and common areas, while the central section is composed of 4 double bedrooms with personal bathrooms.

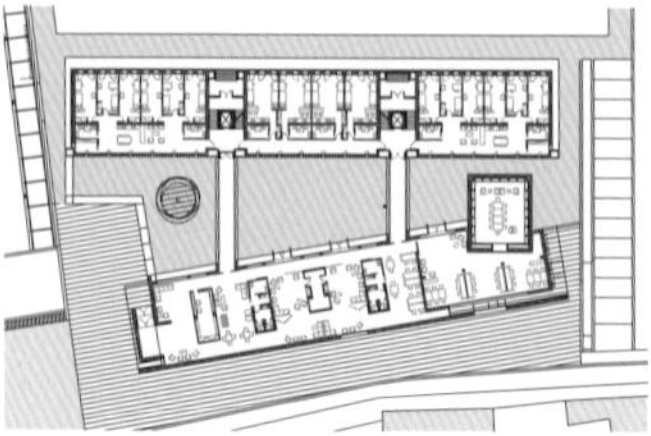

architects
Ipostudio, Paolo Felli,
Massimo Gennari

type
residential

construction
2002-2013

45. Church of San Giovanni Battista, called "Chiesa dell'Autostrada"

Via di Limite
50013, Campi Bisenzio

open to the public

+39 055 421 9016

131R/R003 > Firenze Nuova

Commonly referred to as the "Chiesa dell'Autostrada" because of its location at the crossroads of the Autostrade del Sole and Firenze-Mare motorways, this Church was built to remember the victims of work accidents during the construction of this huge highway infrastructure.
Michelucci proposed highly innovative architecture for that period; a religious building with a complex form that recalled Noah's ark, trees, and a desert tent, without focusing on any element. He overcame the concept of a façade with a lengthwise layout accompanied by a side narthex or entrance, and a curved aisle leading to the Baptistery. Set among the three main areas are two small cloisters planted with olive trees that provide more light to the interior. They create a pause in the tension of the structure and recall the environment in which the church was built. The tree theme is repeated in the internal design where a dense group of reinforced concrete tree-shaped columns rise from thick trunks that branch out to support the roof "tent" rising over the main altar. Different types of stone form the base and flooring alongside exposed concrete slab and walls. Sinuous copper roof panels soar upwards, and walls are punctuated with long vertical windows.

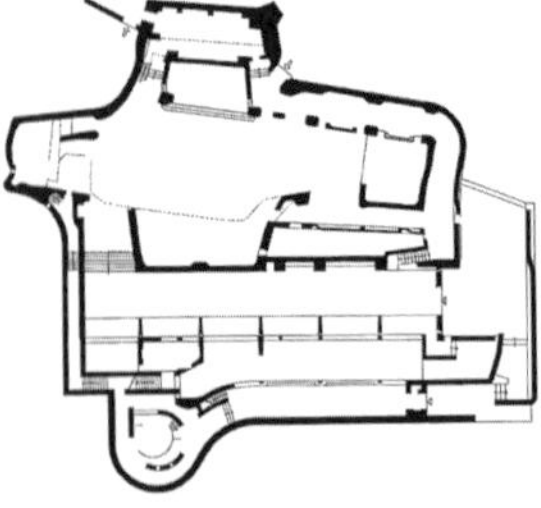

architects
Giovanni Michelucci

type
church

construction
1961-1964

46. Restoration - BP Studio

Piazza Marconi 1
50019, Sesto Fiorentino

external viewing only

www.bpstudio.it

29/66 > Marconi

The aim of this project was to invent a new, highly environmentally, sustainable outer shell for an existing industrial building that now houses the plant and showroom of BP Studio spa.

The simple distribution layout allowed for wide margins for evolution from a functional viewpoint: the large production area on the ground floor was considered as a single space, with adaptable partitions that can subdivide the area according to necessity. Above this, on the upper floor, is a long, central parallelepiped volume containing the management and working office spaces.

The external shell, or new skin, is composed of a material that is both ancient and modern and echoes local traditions. New technology was used: 54,000 Imprunetino terracotta modules were arranged and attached to metal supports to form a contemporary external design. Terracotta is a material able to communicate warmth and territorial identity, durability over time, solidity, and because of its versatile plasticity, can be used to create solid massive surfaces that are gradually lightened to form almost transparent ventilated walls designed to provide the most efficient sustainable energy results.

architects
Claudio Nardi Architects

type
industrial, retail

construction
1999-2001

47. Meeting Point Centre

Via Arturo Chiari 2-8
50127, Florence

external viewing only

131R > Firenze Peretola Aeroporto

Located at the northern-most tip of the city limits, close to the Amerigo Vespucci Airport and A11 motorway, the Meeting Point was conceived as part of the 2000 Jubilee celebrations. The project was designed to reflect the figurative identity of Tuscan architecture, associating the landscape with the concept of the urban Florentine loggia.
Positioned in an area surrounded by important infrastructures, but also closely linked with local traditional rural communities, the building was created as an initial impact to welcome visitors arriving from other destinations, as well as representing a meeting point, providing information, meeting rooms, office spaces, secretarial services, restaurant, and other facilities, spread over two floors. The centre also includes a green planted area and ample parking. The structure is divided into three blocks: two long parallel buildings are set beneath a common flat roof, while a double height portico alongside provides a public rest area and walkway.
The structure is built in reinforced concrete, with cavity brick walls clad in stone slab. The continuous façade cladding and window frames are in African Doussie wood. Windows are in green double glazed Antelio glass, while the buildings are roofed in copper coated wooden strips.

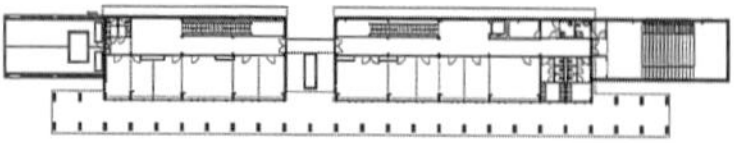

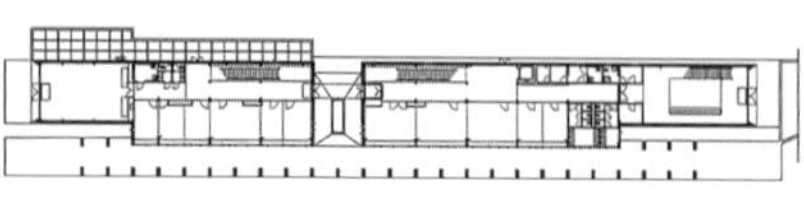

architects
Fabrizio Rossi Prodi,
Francesco Re, Fabio Terrosi

type
multi-purpose building

construction
1998-2000

48. Le Navi Housing

Via Liguria, Via Marche, Via della Sala
50145, Florence

external viewing only

35 > Pistoiese 20

Although it was conceived in the 1960s as a model in social housing, because of its unusual design, the complex, Le Navi, was not built until the mid-1980s, during a sudden need for more residential buildings. The five structures (two overlooking Via Liguria, one in Via Marche, and the other two in Via della Sala), contained 640 apartments in six-storeyed buildings about 200 metres long. Each building was composed of a central distribution corridor, gallery balconies, and large stepped terraces at each end. The prefabricated on-site construction, probably built too quickly, using low quality materials, led to rapid structural decline. Structural damage, electrical and plumbing deterioration, infiltrations, and condensation, combined with considerable changes in living requirements, led to the need for global interventions for renovation work, reconstruction, and installation replacement. In 2001, the Florence city council decided to recover the two buildings in Via Liguria and to redevelop the surrounding urban areas. As well as maintenance, renewal, partial reconstruction and upgrading to current standards of all the existing apartments and façades, the renovation project was able to create 32 new apartments.

architects
Sogene spa / Roberto Melosi - Ufficio ERP Comune di Firenze, Ipostudio (restoration)

type
residential

construction
1982-1986 (construction)
2003-2009 (restoration)

49. Indiano Bridge Viaduct

Viadotto del Ponte all'Indiano
50142, Florence

open to the public

🚌 **5** > L'Indiano
9 > Argin Grosso Canova

The Indiano Bridge connects the Peretola and Isolotto districts at the point where the Mugnone River flows into the Arno. The name stems from the funerary monument near the bridge, erected in honour of the Indian prince, Rajaram Chuttraputti of Kolhapur, who died in Florence in 1870.
The bridge was built according to the winning competition design by architects Adriano Montemagni and Paolo Sica and engineer Fabrizio de Miranda. It is composed of a dual carriageway, double-lane, high-speed roadway. The unusual feature of the design was the concept of a suspended pedestrian walkway that provides a "slow" link-up between the two neighbourhoods, creating a "two level" bridge.
The bridge has a span of over 210 metres, necessary because of the hydrological requirements of the site with the confluence of two rivers. The structure has no piers in the river bed, and, compared to traditional bridges, has a more slender structure and a greater height above the water level. This provides an unobstructed view and represents a strongly emblematic element as an entrance to the city.

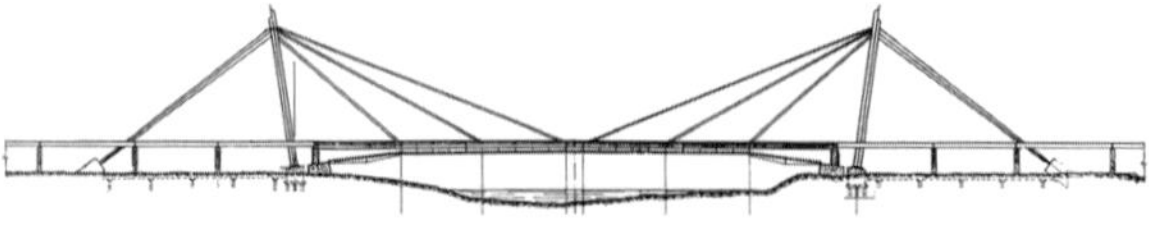

architects
Adriano Montemagni, Paolo Sica, Fabrizio de Miranda

type
bridge

construction
1972-1978

50. Isolotto Quarter

Area between Lungarno dei Pioppi, Via Torcicoda, Via dei Mortuli
50142, Florence

open to the public

T1 > Talenti

9 > Toricoda

The Isolotto began as a village built by INA casa in the 1950s to satisfy the need for post-war housing. The first apartments were delivered in 1954, and the project continued until 1960 providing a total of 1450 apartments. The mayor of Florence, Giorgio La Pira, wanted to build a self-sufficient "satellite town", well-equipped with public services. However, transport connections to Florence city centre, schools, and community centres were not achieved for many years.
The selected area was part of an expansion program, established by urban planning, but without an implementation project. In 1950 INA casa assigned the project to the architects, Pastorini, Pellegrini, Poggi and Tiezzi who created private and shared green spaces between houses, public areas as part of neighbourhood blocks, and a public green space that crossed the entire locality in orthogonal directions. Later Bellucci, Del Debbio, Di Castro, Fagnoni, Gambassi, Gamberini, Michelucci, Pagani and Vaccaro also participated in the project, creating a wide range of residential buildings in a quite highly-populated locality with buildings that did not exceed four floors, with the rare exception of a few six-storey constructions.
In 2014, the town council launched a competition, won by Rossiprodi Associati, to redevelop the public space of Piazza dell'Isolotto.

architects
Raffaello Fagnoni, Italo Gamberini, Giovanni Michelucci

type
residential

construction
1950-1958

51. Scandicci Civic Centre

Piazzale della Resistenza 1
50018, Scandicci

open to the public

+39 055 7591320
www.comune.scandicci.fi.it
urp@comune.scandicci.fi.it

T1 > Resistenza

26/61/62/63/83/ 94/M/S1 > Francoforte sull'Oder

The new Scandicci Civic Centre is part of a wider masterplan commissioned in 2003 from Rogers Stirk Harbour + Partners to transform a large area in the suburbs of Florence changing it from a satellite town to a new vibrant town centre. The proposed solution is composed of a public square flanked by several buildings and includes a new tram station linking Scandicci with the Florence city centre. The project involves both public and private sectors based on the concept that a truly active public space is used by a vast range of people in the community.
The contemporary architectural style is aimed at creating a harmonious concept for the entire complex, rather than on each individual building. The complex is composed of a cultural centre, a commercial building, and a residential apartment building. The ground floor of all buildings has been assigned to retail stores.
Rogers Stirk Harbour + Partners have adopted a strongly sustainable approach for this intervention, a concept they apply to all their projects. Solar panels and solar elements, green roofing on the cultural centre, and the focus on the tram station, aimed at encouraging the community to use public transport.

© Rogers Stirk Harbour + Partners

architects
Rogers Stirk Harbour + Partners, Studio DA, Erika Skabar (landscape)

type
multi-purpose centre

construction
2008-2014

52. Military Aviation Institute

Viale dell'Aeronautica 14
50144, Florence

external viewing only

www.aeronautica.difesa.it

17 > Le Cascine

The current Military Aviation Institute is located within the Parco delle Cascine, in an area also used for a target shooting range and home to an experimental arboretum. The complex, which was constructed in less than a year, maintains all its original aspects: buildings, furnishings, decor, and its beautifully landscaped surroundings. Considered a masterpiece of Italian Rationalistic architecture, the complex is composed of various blocks around the fulcrum, or Command Centre. The complex has a quadrangular layout, around a central courtyard, with "bridge" corridor structures linking opposite buildings, leaving an open view at ground level. The complex includes the training school building – an L-shaped "comb" structure, aeronautics and thermodynamics pavilion, airmen's barracks and service buildings, sports facilities and officers' quarters. An interesting chiaroscuro effect is created by the apartments on the two upper floors, positioned slantwise to the façade.
All buildings, constructed in reinforced concrete, are faced in brick with travertine cornices, except for the gym and swimming pool, finished with a white lime render. The interior decor includes mosaic elements, marble floors, and decorations by Bruno Catarzi, Mario Moschi, Giovanni Colacicchi, Pietro Annigoni and Luigi Gori.

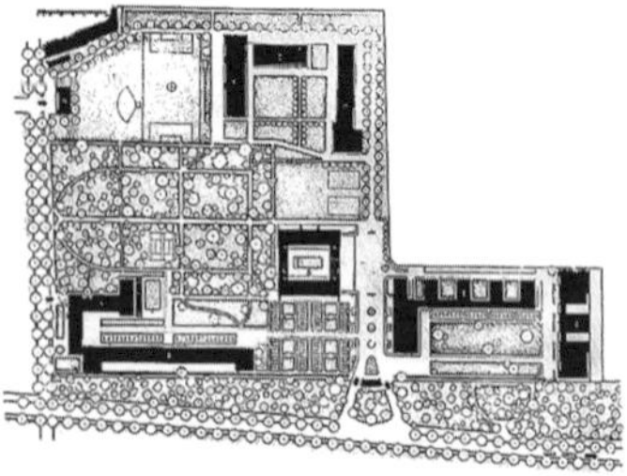

architects
Raffaello Fagnoni

type
school

construction
1936-1938

53. Opera Theatre

Piazzale Vittorio Gui 1
50144, Florence

+39 055 2779309

www.operadifirenze.it

T1 > Porta al Prato - Leopolda

29/30/35/57 > Stazione Leopolda

Positioned at the crossroads between the historic city centre, the Parco delle Cascine, and the nearby Leopoldina Station, the opera theatre represents the most important musical cultural centre in Florence.
The building is composed of three music rooms, two auditoriums, and an open-air amphitheatre. A sloping pedestrian walkway crosses the nearby Macinante canal linking the amphitheatre with the park. The roofing is composed of a series of sloping lines that overlap one another to create an open-air ramp that rises upwards, guiding spectators to the amphitheatre with an audience capacity of 2,000; it continues towards a panoramic viewing platform. The façade of the large sloped base containing the two music rooms, includes the vast 35-metre stage tower. The cladding and facing materials contribute to the sober elegance of the architectural design: the external façades are in green-blue enamelled brick and unglazed porcelain tiles, with pear wood for perfect acoustics within the building. A fixed brick sun screen structure was dry-mounted on the stage tower using mechanical anchoring systems attached to aluminium frames and steel beams to create a light shimmering effect of solids and voids. The external surfaces of the music rooms are composed of large thin unglazed porcelain sheets, glued directly onto the structure framework.

© ABDR Architetti Associati

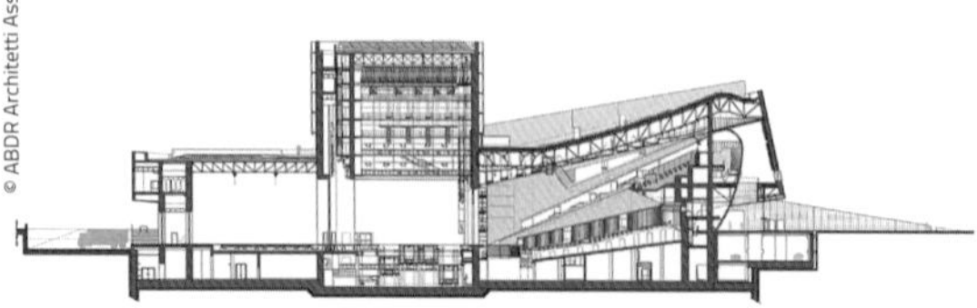

architects
ABDR Architetti Associati

type
theatre

construction
2008-2011

54. Entrance Piazza to the ex Leopolda Station

Viale Fratelli Rosselli 5
50144, Florence

open to the public only during specific events

+39 055 212622
info@stazione-leopolda.com
www.stazione-leopolda.com

T1 > Porta al Prato - Leopolda

29/30/35/57 > Stazione Leopolda

The Leopolda Station is the former railway station of Porta al Prato, the terminus of the oldest Grand duchy railway line (Florence-Pisa-Livorno), called Leopolda in honour of the Grand Duke Leopold. It was opened in 1848. The station was decommissioned as early as 1860 when the line was re-routed to the Maria Antonia Station (now Santa Maria Novella). The former Leopolda Station underwent many changes over the years: it hosted the first National Exhibition after the unification of Italy, the Customs and Excise headquarters during the period Florence was capital of Italy, a bullet manufacturing plant, and a rolling stock repair shop, until the bombings in 1944.

In the '90s, the centre section was converted as a space for exhibitions, fairs, and events for the fashion business. In 2008, the new Porta al Prato station was opened on the right-hand side of the exhibition space. Gae Aulenti's project for the piazza in front of the former Leopolda Station highlights the main access through the addition of internal structural elements within the open space. Steel columns emphasise the lengthwise perspective and the transversal structures create the effect of a pergola, a space to pause, an entrance hall.

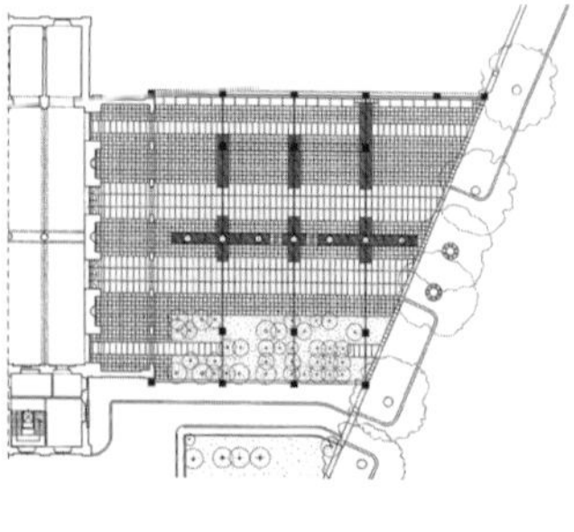

© Archivio Gae Aulenti

architects
Gae Aulenti, Bianca Ballestrero

type
multi-purpose space

construction
1989

55. Ex Singer Building

Via Cittadella 7
50144, Florence

external viewing only

+39 055 3200800

23 > Viale Fratelli Rosselli 66

This two-storey building in Via Cittadella, has a well-balanced and harmonious façade, both for its formal design and the materials employed. The ground floor has five rectangular windows placed at the side of the main entrance, while the upper floor has a row of ten openings, two for each of the lower floor windows. The long, narrow, ground floor openings are arranged in a regular pattern. This composition is flanked by the entrance on the left, with a cross-framed window above, and a vehicle entrance on the right. The façade is clad with terracotta tiles, an unusual material for Florentine architecture, where a rendered plaster finish is more common.

The building has a trapezoidal floor plan. The ground floor houses the technical utility rooms, while the office space is on the upper floor. As well as the design and project management, the architect also created the internal design. The materials are of high quality: large yellow marble slabs for the flooring, white marble and polished brass for the entrance staircase, ivory painted walls and wooden furnishings.

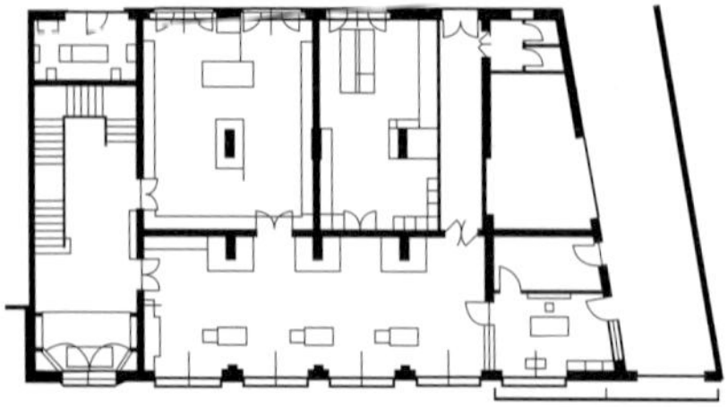

architects
Italo Gamberini

type
offices

construction
1937-1938

56. San Jacopino Condominium

Piazza San Jacopino 5B
50127, Florence

external viewing only

22/23/57 >
Maragliano
San Jacopino
23 > Ponte all'Asse

This building is renowned for its irregular shape created through the intersection of different volumes: the triangular prism of the main staircase overlooking Piazza San Jacopino, the rectangular and cylindrical forms of the apartment units, horizontally punctuated with recessed and projecting elements, and the cylindrical form of the secondary staircases. The complex assembly can also be seen in the square modules that have been rotated by 45 degrees compared to the unit below to create void spaces between one floor and another. The layout is based on this juxtaposition of three groups of apartments, positioned around their respective stair wells. The apartments themselves have quite a traditional floorplan divided into living and sleeping zones. The ground floor, conceived as a glass-walled base, has spacious areas destined for retail stores.
Colour plays an important role in this construction: the contrast between the red-brown render and the lime green window frames underlines the interrupted lines and intersections of the different volumes.

architects
Marco Dezzi Bardeschi

type
residential

construction
1973-1976

57. Evergreen University Student Residence

Piazza Luigi Dallapiccola 1
50144, Florence

external viewing only

+39 055 3245386
info@evergreenimmobiliare.it
www.evergreenimmobiliare.it/site/home.asp

56/60 > Dallapiccola

The complex is composed of a student residential block, public piazza, and garage, and was built on the area of the former wood panel manufacturing plant, Artieri del legno, located in an urban area previously occupied by production plants, many of which have been demolished. The demolition of the ex-plant produced a plot of approximately 7,000 square metres, providing the space for a large residence, seven floors above ground, and two basement floors. The two basement floors are connected to the piazza behind the building, and contain 370 parking spaces and garages, plus a work-out gym. The ground floor is divided into public service offices, and the upper floors provide 132 student rooms and apartments, designed in different modules, each room containing 1, 2, 3, or 4 beds. These apartments have views from three sides of the building; on the western side they overlook a large, slightly concave piazza strongly integrated with the building, since it is completely open from the interior, and is protected by a large overhead shade roof plus two projecting side wings. Externally, as well as the monochromatic white colour, a main feature is the system of painted metal sun break strips, designed to protect against direct sunlight and guarantee greater privacy.

architects
Studio di Architettura Galli e Gueli

type
residential

construction
2001-2002

58. Ex Tobacco Plant and Puccini Theatre

Ex Tobacco Plant:
Via delle Cascine 35
Puccini Theatre:
Via delle Cascine 41
50144, Florence

Ex Tobacco Plant:
external viewing only

Puccini Theatre:
open to the public only
during performances
Ticket office hours
Thu - Fri - Sat / 4 pm - 7 pm
+39 055 362067
info@teatropuccini.it
www.teatropuccini.it

17 > Tartini 01

The complex is composed of several tobacco production buildings and the current Puccini Theatre positioned on the corner.
Built following the relocation of the previous plant from the former Church of San Pancrazio, which now houses the Museo Marino Marini, the production plant which was active between 1940 and 2001 – was designed in 1934 as a group of Rationalist style buildings in an urban block near the Parco delle Cascine. On a long slightly concave band, faced with slabs of travertine that highlight the monumental aspect of the entrance façade, are three bas-relief works by the sculptor, Francesco Coccia. They were designed as decorative panels for the balustrades that divide the three wide window openings on the façade, and portray the cultivation, production and sale of tobacco.
The Cinema Teatro, built in 1940 as a recreation space for the tobacco plant workers, occupies the North-East corner facing Piazza Puccini. The symmetrical rounded façade, also clad with travertine, coherent with the adjacent buildings, features a wide staircase with a large central bas-relief panel by the same artist. This is aligned with the tall tower in concrete and glass, reminiscent of the Maratona tower at the Franchi sports stadium.

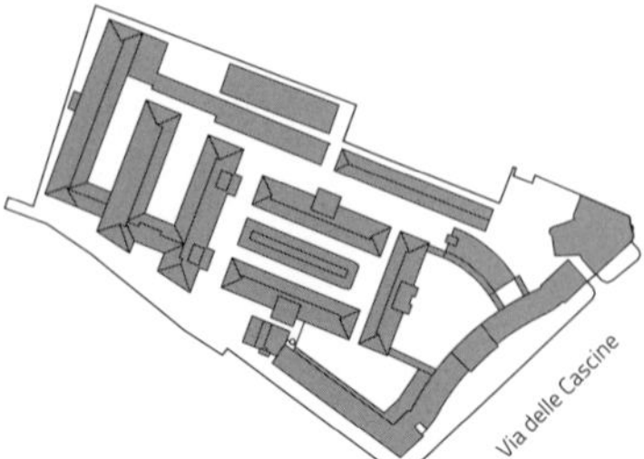

architects
Ufficio Tecnico del
Monopolio di Stato

type
multi-purpose space, theatre

construction
1933-1940

59. Novoli Quarter

Via di Novoli, Via Enrico Forlanini, Viale Guidoni, Via della Toscana
50127, Florence

open to the public

57/70 > Villaggio Forlanini
5 > Piccagli

Novoli, in the North-West of Florence, is one of the districts which has undergone some of the largest urban transformations in recent decades. In the 1930s, 32 hectares were occupied by the FIAT plant for vehicle repairs. The plant was closed in the 1980s, and since that time a series of different projects have been proposed for the area. The current layout of the district is the project proposed in 1994 by Leon Krier, who was strongly in favour of redefining European suburban areas based on historicist models. The Law Court was maintained in its central position, but pedestrian zones, low buildings, and intimate public spaces were arranged around the Court. The restoration implementation plan was assigned to Gabetti and Isola. Isolarchitetti later designed the park space, the Urban Center, converted from the former power station, a multi-function building, and four urban blocks for housing and retail stores. The buildings were designed with varying heights and included porticos, loggias and overhead connections for shelter.
Natalini Architetti was charged with designing the Socio-Economic and Law Faculties. C+S designed the student accommodation which, while respecting the limits imposed by the urban plan, differs from the other buildings in style, with a more compact design, as do the two residential blocks by Claudio Nardi.
The large park connects this area with the Law Court (60) and the headquarters of the Cassa di Risparmio di Firenze (61), also included in this book.

architects
Leon Krier, Isolarchitetti, Natalini Architetti, C+S, Claudio Nardi Architects

type
residential, retail, university

construction
1994-2011

60. Florence Law Courts

Viale Alessandro Guidoni 61
50127, Florence

January - December
Mon - Fri / 8 am - 7.15 pm
Sat / 8 am - 2.30 pm
Sun / closed

+39 055 79941

www.tribunale.firenze.giustizia.it

5/22 > Nuovo Palazzo di Giustizia
5 > Guidoni

This complex contains all the administrative offices that were previously located in several buildings in the Florence city centre: the Law Courts, the Public Prosecutor's office, Municipal Court, and the Court of Appeal. In 1987, the city council commissioned Leonardo Ricci and Giovanni Michelucci to draw up a project based on clear guidelines: the main axis of the complex led to the historic centre of the city, with a central route that was based on the concept of a public space like a street or piazza. The following year, Michelucci abandoned the project, which was assigned to Ricci and the engineer, Giorgio Santucci. The preliminary project was completed in 1988, but construction did not begin until 2000, with an interruption between 2006 and 2008 – six years after Ricci's death. The imposing construction covers an area of 130,000 square metres. The Law Courts is built around a courtyard with nineteen floors above ground, and two underground. The façades are elaborate and feature a three-dimensional effect: sloping walls and volumes that emerge from the building's façades, as well as a range of materials including Santa Fiora stone cladding, glass and solar panels.

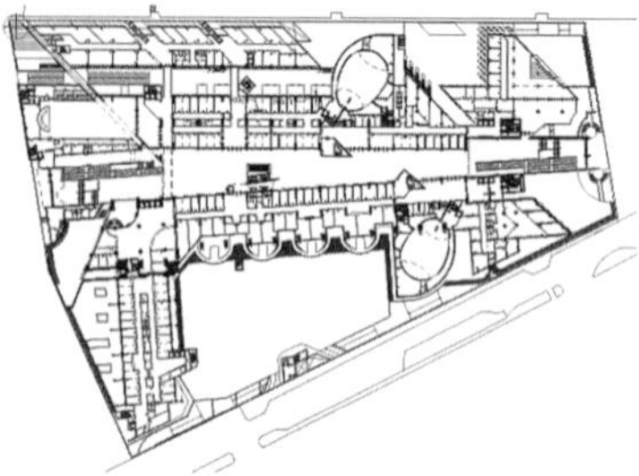

architects
Leonardo Ricci, Giorgio Santucci

type
courthouse, offices

construction
1987-2012

61. Cassa di Risparmio di Firenze Building

Via Carlo Magno 3
50127, Florence

external viewing only

+39 055 2613758

5/22 > Nuovo Palazzo di Giustizia

In 2004, the Cassa di Risparmio di Firenze launched a competition by invitation in which designers were required to respect the town planning guidelines laid out by Leon Krier in 1994 for areas of the former Fiat and Carapelli plants, as well as the variation set out by Paolo Spinelli.
The bank headquarters are housed in one large building with a regular layout: it is composed of a single consistent construction, like a small walled town focussed towards its internal centre. The perimeter walls of the building are punctuated with different openings, continuity elements, interruptions, and passages of different sizes. Each block contains one or two sections, and the various blocks are connected by two-storeyed glazed bridges built entirely in steel.
Inside the garden-courtyard is an auditorium built partially below ground. The windowed upper part, faced with brick, emerges at garden level, and has a stone portico on the south side. The building roof is planted in lawn. The design concept of the walled perimeter is emphasised by the choice of materials: the external façades are clad in sandstone, while the transversal and internal walls are built with facing bricks, except for the portico columns and architraves, which are faced in stone.

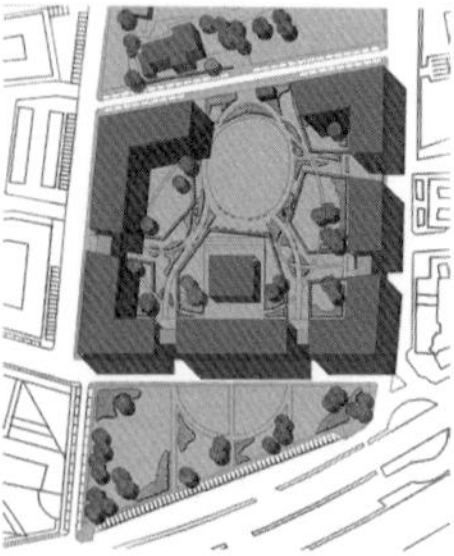

© Giorgio Grassi

architects
Giorgio Grassi, Nunzio Dego, Giorgio Cubeddu, Nicola Cimarosti, Studio Cortinovis-Lameri

type
offices, auditorium

construction
2004-2009

62. Firenze Nova Residential Complex

Via Panciatichi 55
50127, Florence

external viewing only

5/59 > Firenze Nova

Previously an apartment block, this large seven-story building is set in the new district of Firenze Nova, a residential and corporate zone in the North-West of the city; it has now been converted into a prestigious residential complex. According to the urban redevelopment plan, the internal layout was transformed without changing the support structures. The building was divided into a series of duplex apartments as well as smaller sized single floor apartments. By remodelling the internal dividing partitions, it was possible to obtain a total of 145 units, composed of single and double roomed apartments, with triple roomed units in the corners.

The building was clad with a steel structure to support a system of wide loggia screens in an irregular pattern, using perforated panels of various sizes. This solution provides sun screening as well as acting as a sound barrier and gives the façade a distinctive design. The asymmetrical screen panel patterns are composed of dry-assembled white enamelled terracotta elements, designed by Archea in collaboration with the artist, Franco Ionda.

The ground floor is occupied by retail stores and two entrances to the residential floors above. It features a continuous glazed surface that conceals the constructive block's contact with the ground, making it seem lighter and less entrenched.

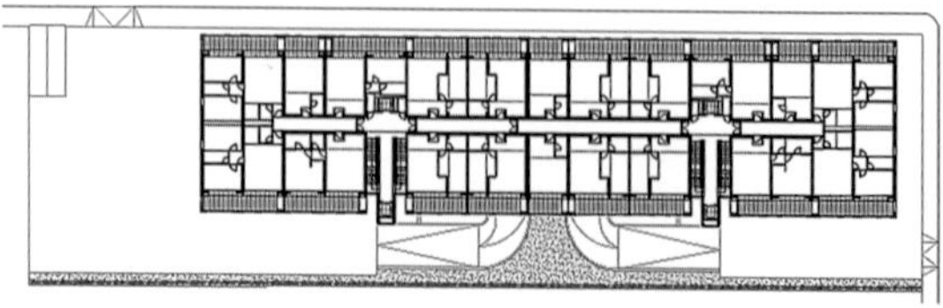

architects
Archea Associati

type
residential

construction
2006-2011

0 m
100 m
300 m
Via Edmondo de Amicis
Via Lungo l'Affrico
Via Giuseppe Sirtori
Via Castelfidardo
Via P. Maroncelli
Via Manfredo Fanti
Via M. Amari
Viale Manfredo Fanti
Via Enrico Cialdini
Via Andrea del Sarto
Via Bernardo Ramazzini
Viale Edmondo de Amicis
Via Milazzo
Via Marsala
Via delle Cento Stelle
Via Pasquale Paoli
Viale Manfredo Fanti
Viale Pierluigi Nervi
Stadio Artemio Franchi
68
Via S. Gervasio
Via Malta
Via Pier F. Calvi
Via F.lli Bandiera
Via del Campo D'Arrigo
Via E. Rubieri
Via Aurelio Saffi
Via Goffredo Mameli
Via Giovanni Duprè
Viale dei Mille
Via Frusa
Via Mannelli
Via Fra' Paolo Sarpi
Via dei Sette Santi
Via Alessandro Marchetti
65
64
Via Masaccio
Via Gian Battista Vico
Via Ciro Menotti
Stazione Campo di Marte
FS
Via Antonio Scialoia
Via Giuseppe Mazzini
Via Benedetto Varchi
Via Jacopo Nardi
Via E. Repetti
66
Via Giovanni Bovio
Via G. Marconi
Via del Pratellino
Via Giuseppe la Farina
Via Giambologna
Via Andrea Castagno
Via Francesco Domenico Guerrazzi
Via dei Della Robbia
Via C. Botta
Via Pietro Colletta
Viale Antonio Gr
5
6
I
J

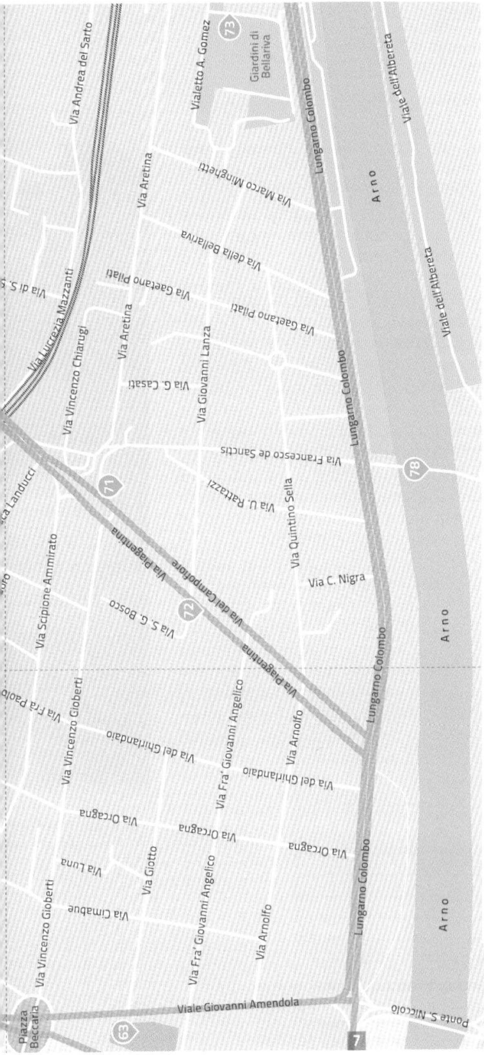

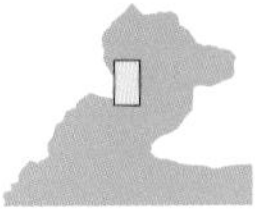

Florence South-East

63. State Archives Building
64. Mandragora Publisher
65. Church of Sacro Cuore
66. Apartments in Via Guerrazzi
67. Ex Nuova Italia Building
68. Artemio Franchi Municipal Stadium
69. Monterinaldi Residential Complex
70. Resortis Residential Complex
71. Shopping Centre, Student Residence, Parking
72. Apartments in Via Piagentina
73. RAI Headquarters
74. La Rotonda Pavilion
75. Church of San Giuseppe Artigiano
76. Rovezzano Quarter
77. Sorgane Quarter
78. Giovanni da Verrazzano Bridge
79. Emergency service 118 - Piero Palagi Hospital
80. Abbey of San Miniato al Monte
81. Villa Bayon
82. Misericordia Cemetery Extension
83. Ugolino Golf Club
84. Autostrada del Sole Acoustic Barriers

63. State Archives Building

Viale della Giovine Italia 6
50122, Florence

January - December
Mon - Fri / 8.30 am - 5.30 pm
Sat / 8.30 am -1.45 pm
Sun / closed

+39 055 263201

www.archiviodistato.firenze.it

8/12/31/81 > Gioberti

Located in the Uffizi palace until 1988, plans had been made to transfer the State Archives following the terrible floods in 1966. The new building was constructed on a plot that had housed the Casa della Gioventù Italiana del Littorio – designed by Aurelio Cetica – where about a century earlier, Giuseppe Poggi had created the large ring road around the city. The project won a competition in 1971, which included the demolition of the previous building.
Construction began in 1977, and the building was inaugurated on February 4th, 1989. The reinforced concrete structure is clad entirely with artificial stone panels. The complex is composed of two long blocks connected by an internal street leading from viale Duca degli Abruzzi to piazza Beccaria; organised as an exhibition space, the internal street can be used independently from the Archive building, creating an ideal connection with the city. The staggered building south of this axis is composed of six to eight different levels and contains the document storage departments. The building on the north side, divided into two sections on five and six levels, features a glazed walkway overlooking the street, and is reserved for work spaces, including a study room with overhead skylights. The two buildings are connected by suspended walkways positioned at various levels.

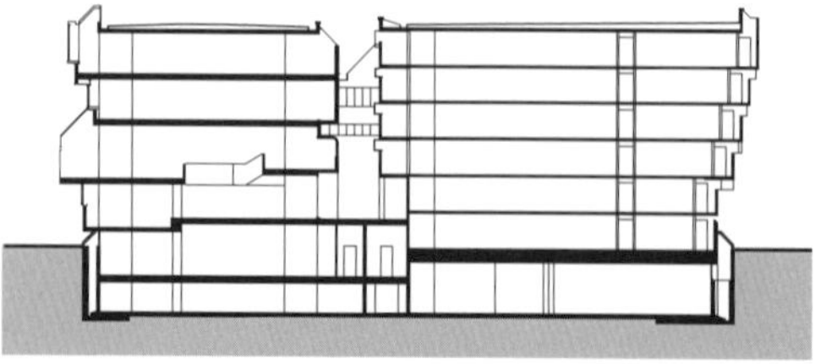

architects
Italo Gamberini, Loris Macci, Rino Vernuccio, Franco Bonaiuti

type
archive, offices

construction
1971-1989

64. Mandragora Publisher

Via Capo di Mondo 61
50136, Florence

external viewing only

+39 055 2654384
info@mandragora.it
www.mandragora.it

6 > Oberdan

The new headquarters of the Mandragora publishing house is located in the centre of a 19th and 20th century urban neighbourhood which previously housed local craft workshops, traces of which can still be found.
The new building, visible from street level through the transparent entrance into the first courtyard, is positioned crosswise to the roadway within an irregular shape dictated by the boundaries of the plot. A first courtyard, reserved for parking, is flanked by a long rectangular building containing the entrance and office spaces. A second entrance at the end of the courtyard leads to a C-shaped structure, enhanced with a second courtyard surrounded by the three wings of the building. The two blocks, interrupted with voids and tangent planes on floors at different levels, rediscover spatial continuity in the basement and upper floors, where a raised walkway links both buildings and provides access to the roof terrace.
A solid concrete base supports light transparent structures in glass and steel, creating pleasant light-filled work spaces, enhanced by the dynamic but functional effect of open communication, necessary among the various work spaces.

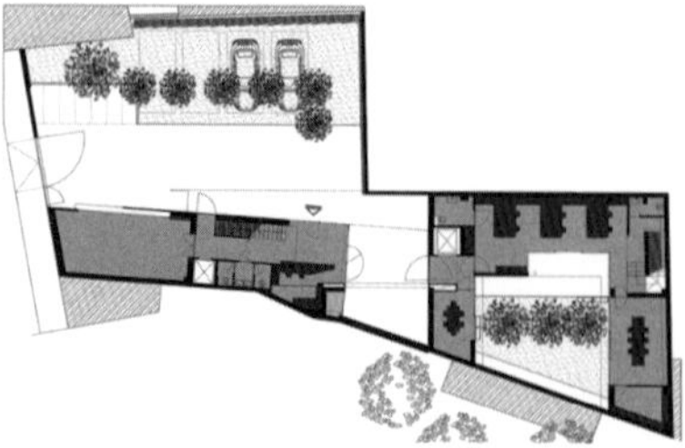

architects
Claudio Nardi Architects

type
offices

construction
2009-2013

65. Church of Sacro Cuore

Via Capo di Mondo 60
50136, Florence

open to the public

+39 055 670148
info@sacrocuore.firenze.it
www.sacrocuore.firenze.it

6 > Oberdan

The Church of Sacro Cuore, constructed between 1874 and 1877, underwent considerable restructuration work in the 1950s. The project was designed by the architect, Lando Bartoli, and the engineer, Lisandro Baldassini collaborated with Pier Luigi Nervi for the structural project.
The church is the expression of a place of worship with a modern interpretation using exposed reinforced concrete in the façade and structure. This project reinterprets the concept of the façade and bell-tower typical of certain Gothic churches together with the strong tall spire. This work shows the careful attention that Bartoli paid to the urban planning aspect of the intervention: the bell tower provides a reference point, a recognisable element, and the focal point at the end of an important Florentine street.
The interior of the church reveals more traditional solutions when compared to the innovative impact of the façade. The floorplan has three naves and, like the exterior, the structure has been left clearly visible. In the plain sober decor, the large stained glass window of the Resurrection by Marcello Avenali, at the entrance, is particularly striking.

architects
Lando Bartoli

type
church

construction
1956-1962

66. Apartments in Via Guerrazzi

Via Guerrazzi 6-8
50132, Florence

external viewing only

This building is composed of a small number of apartments, each with a different layout. The style is more like a detached house than an apartment building, beginning with the curved staircase. The layout of each floor is offset, in comparison to the one above, and the living space increases with each level.
Spadolini's design style is clearly visible in his careful attention to the external facings; he used wall panels in reinforced concrete cast on concave semi-cylindrical formwork. The panels are used to underline the offset bands that indicate each floor, where windows and loggias seem to have been positioned in a somewhat random fashion. Window frames are in wood, and the curved balustrades, that recall the curved facing panels, are in copper.

6/12/19 > Mazzini 01

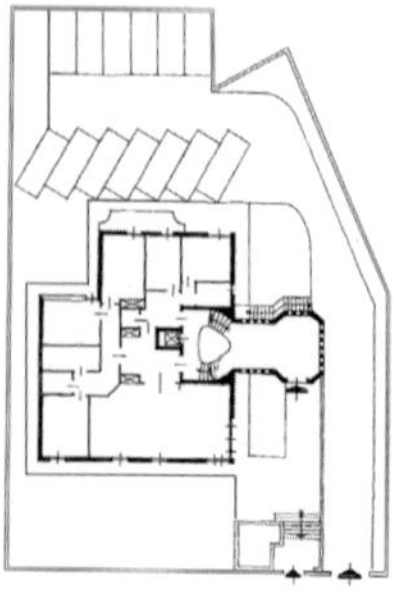

architects
Pierluigi Spadolini

type
residential

construction
1968-1969

67. Ex Nuova Italia Building

Via Giacomini 8
50132, Florence

external viewing only

+39 055 27831

10/11/17/20/ 52/54 > Savonarola

This building was designed for the headquarters of the Nuova Italia publishing house, commissioned by the director at that time, Ernesto Codignola; today it houses the offices of the prefecture.
The designer, Edoardo Detti, worked in collaboration with Carlo Scarpa as consultant, and with Luigi Caldarelli, Gianfranco Dallerba and Paolo Donati.
The complex is composed of two buildings; the main structure overlooks via Giacomini, and the other, over the parallel street, via Fattori. The first building has a stone base and a semi-transparent portico on the ground floor. On the first, third and fourth floors, the exposed concrete walls are punctuated with tall vertical windows in an irregular pattern. The second-floor façade is recessed back to the support column depth, to create a glazed portico. The sixth floor, set well back from the façade, is not visible from street level. The second structure is similar in style, but only on three levels. Great attention has been paid to detail: the staircase of the main building designed by Carlo Scarpa, and the recessed windows in the façade with slightly smaller external openings to hide the window frames.

architects
Edoardo Detti, Carlo Scarpa

type
offices

construction
1968-1972

68. Artemio Franchi Municipal Stadium

Viale Manfredo Fanti 4
50137, Florence

open to the public only
during sporting events

+39 055 503011

10/20/82/84 >
Fanti Stadio Ridolfi

Initially named after Giovanni Berta and later after Artemio Franchi, the stadium was designed in 1929 by Pierluigi Nervi and built on a former military parade ground.
Recognised as a masterpiece of Italian architecture during the Thirties, and as a symbol of reinforced concrete modernity, the stadium is famous for its monumental entrance, designed by Giuntoli – although no longer used as the main entrance. It also featured modern helical staircases, a projecting cantilevered roof over the terraces, and a tall slender tower designed later by Nervi, in 1931.
Forty years of repeated, unsuccessful interventions and structural decline revealed a need for important renovation and extension work before the 1990 world championships. In 1984, the work was assigned to Italo Gamberini, Loris Macci and collaborators. The project had three objectives: rational design of all services, upgraded accesses and safety systems, increased stadium capacity. As well as the new structural work, all superfluous elements were eliminated, including the former athletics track; the playing field was lowered, and a new internal amphitheatre was built. Two projecting roof covers were added, as well as a gym, an inside swimming pool, internal and external parking, and two pavilions built on each side of the monumental entrance. Two steel staircases were built for safety reasons.

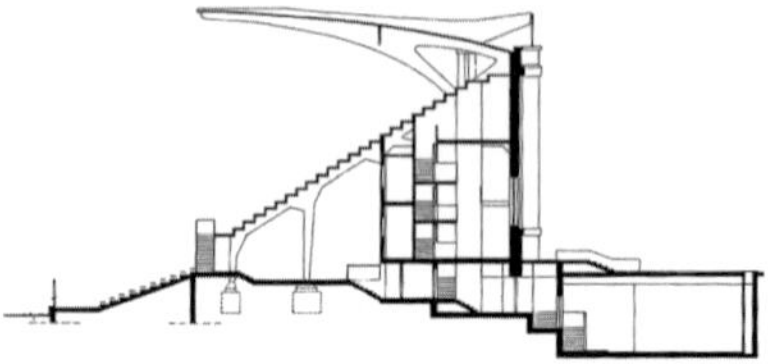

architects
Pierluigi Nervi, Alessandro Giuntoli / Italo Gamberini, Loris Macci (renovation)

type
sports centre

construction
1929-1932
1984-1990 (renovation)

69. Monterinaldi Residential Complex

Via di Monterinaldi
50139, Florence

external viewing only

25 > Bolognese Nuova 03

The village of Monterinaldi is an experimental residential complex composed of 22 independent houses, including the home and studio of the architect Ricci himself, built on an old former quarry on the Monterinaldi headland opposite Fiesole, a few kilometres from Florence.
The planning scheme was based on an "open" program amenable to changes and integrations, and at the same time, to a dialogue between the buildings and the complex orographical nature of the area. The position of each building was conditioned by the terrain, while capturing the best panoramic views and sunlight. Despite the homogeneous architectural style, there is great variety in the distribution and spatial layouts where the influence of Lloyd Wright's organic design is obvious in the structural composition and the symbiotic relationship with the natural surroundings. The compenetration of internal and external spaces is unconventional, with fluid, but dynamic movement between spaces arranged on different levels, intersecting in different ways; volumes are divided by irregular openings and oblique planes eliminate any type of hierarchy among the various elements. The contrasting materials have strong impact: exposed local sandstone walls are combined with neoplastic structures in reinforced concrete, render finish, glass, wood and metal.

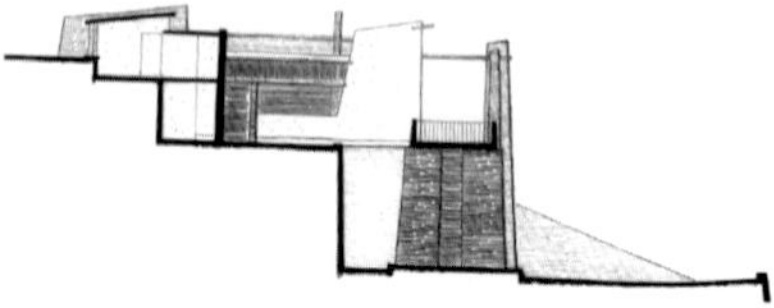

© Sara Benzi

architects
Leonardo Ricci, Gianfranco Petrelli, Giovanni Klaus Koenig

type
residential

construction
1949-1964

70. Resortis Residential Complex

Via Portigiani 72
50014, Fiesole

external viewing only

🚌 **7/45/47** > Fiesole Piazza Mino

In 2005, redevelopment work began on the plot of the former Macelli plant, in the historic centre of Fiesole, a complex zone for its position in the urban fabric and for the steeply sloping terrain. As well as residential buildings, the urban redevelopment plan included a parking area and the widening of the road surface in via Sermei.

The project designed by Pietro Carlo Pellegrini provides 22 apartments in a single building divided into three staggered blocks with different heights and layout. In this way, the construction follows the curves and levels of the terrain; it is composed of three floors above ground and one basement level for personal parking space. The dynamic structural pattern is repeated in the façades with the staggered window openings.

The building structure is in reinforced concrete, with a traditional rendered finish in a cement and earth pigment mix, and sloping roofs covered with Tuscan terracotta tiles to blend with this historic context of considerable importance.

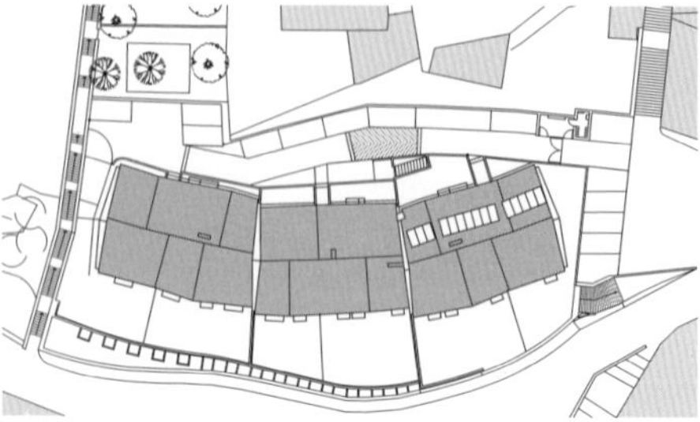

architects
Pietro Carlo Pellegrini

type
residential

construction
2005-2010

71. Shopping Centre, Student Residence, Parking

Piazza Alberti, Via Campofiore
50100, Florence

open to the public

3/14/82 > Alberti 03
3/82 > Alberti 04

This project occupies an area occupied by the former ATAF deposit in Piazza Alberti; it is part of a newly redeveloped complex composed of a multi-storey carpark, shopping centre, student residence, park, and piazza.
The main objective was a redevelopment scheme to integrate leisure spaces with certain sensorial elements suggested by the context: light, shade, visual filters, textured weave, interlocking and connection, and colour contrasts. These elements were created through projects focused on texture and composition, like the curved micro-perforated steel panels supported by a tubular structure covering the reinforced concrete frame of the carpark. This creates a dynamic scenographic effect animated by internal motion and lighting. The building base differs from the upper floors recalling traditional Renaissance architecture, with the use of stone, terracotta, and plaster render, used alongside steel, glass and wood elements. The play in vertical and horizontal compositions create passages, visual perspectives, and shafts of light.
The discovery of archaeological finds in the area increased the historical significance of the piazza, with the integration of an exhibition space dedicated to the discoveries. The piazza is organised on two levels, catering to open-air events and exhibitions.

architects
Paolo Di Nardo, Alessandra Ciullini

type
service, residential, parking

construction
2001-2007

72. Apartments in Via Piagentina

Via San Giovanni Bosco 1, corner Via Piagentina 29
50121, Florence

external viewing only

3/14/82 > Piagentina - Negozio Tre

This building sits on a corner plot, with six floors above ground along via Piagentina, and four floors in via San Giovanni Bosco, plus a basement. Savioli applied combined technical and architectural, often quite complex, concepts during the construction stage, but always with original results with great impact. The strong focus on vertical elements, less noticeable today because of ensuing construction in the area, drew its inspiration from the historic Florentine Tower-house. This concept can be seen on the corner occupied by a compact, independent elevator shaft. Attached to the tower are various units with different sizes, configurations, constructive details, and flat or "bi-convex" roofing; composed of repeatable elements they are combined to form layouts that are always different. The same free-flowing composition also exists within the building. There are two apartments on the ground, first, and second floors, while the other floors have a single apartment. The basement contains the garages. Each individual apartment is different from the others, partly due to the use of sliding partitions.
However, the whole building has a coherent style due to the exposed concrete used inside and out, the same prefabricated wood and concrete window and door frames, and the curved corners that provide surface continuity.

architects
Leonardo Savioli, Danilo Santi

type
residential

construction
1964-1967

73. RAI Headquarters

Largo Alcide De Gasperi 1
50136, Florence

external viewing only

+39 055 2488323
firenze.teca.aperta@rai.it

14 > Aretina

The building is an L-shaped structure composed of two blocks connected by a central element containing the entrance hall, stairs and elevators.
Each block houses different departments: the management offices are in the building in the north-south direction, while the other block houses the radio zone. The different activities are also indicated externally with contrasting façade finishes. One building features long horizontal ribbon windows, while the other block, more solid, is divided by a regular exposed steel grid framework.
The architect, Italo Gamberini, took great care with the façade finishes using innovative technologies adapted to a building of this type and context. Pink-ochre Silipol sheets that recall traditional Tuscan colours, were used to clad both buildings, while the horizontal connections and technical utility spaces are faced in grey-blue porcelain coated steel that reflects the colours of the hills in the landscape.

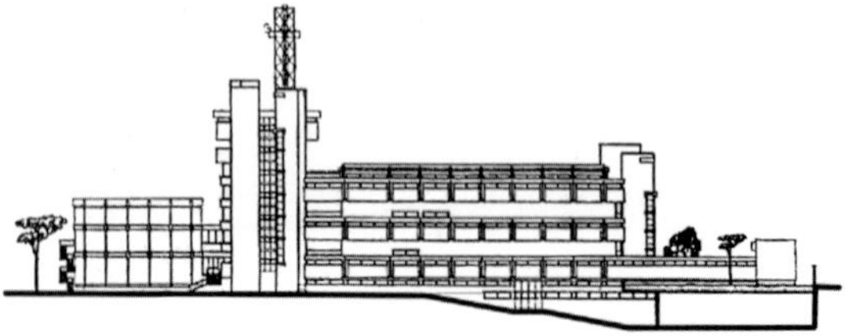

architects
Italo Gamberini, Loris Macci, Antonio Bambi, Luciano Parecchio, Sergio Barsotti

type
offices

construction
1962-1967

74. La Rotonda Pavilion

Piazza Niccolò Tommaseo
50135, Florence

external viewing only

+39 055 697477
settignano@parrocchie.
diocesifirenze.it
www.parrocchiasettignano.it

10 > Settignano

This pavilion was built in answer to a request from the parish priest, for a multi-function space for the local parish. Raffaello Fagnoni was faced with the difficult task of considering the various activities to be held in the space, and of creating an extremely flexible structure, but which was also appropriate in its role as a religious building.
The style of this community building was emphasised by the form itself: a cylindrical volume with a central area able to provide interaction between spectators and spectacle. The structure was built in exposed concrete and brick, two of Fagnoni's favourite materials, and suited to the modest sum available for the construction. The reinforced concrete structure plays a leading role inside the building. The perimeter is composed of a circle of columns that support the seating balcony, and that then branch upwards to sustain the roof ribbing; all concrete elements are exposed. The roof is made of traditional materials and the two rows of glazed windows on the ground and first floors are divided by a band of bricks.

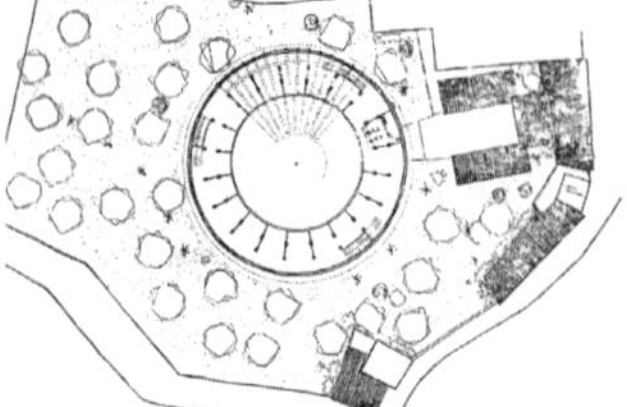

architects
Raffaello Fagnoni

type
parish centre

construction
1961

75. Church of San Giuseppe Artigiano

Via Tre Pini 8
50014, Montebeni

open to the public

+39 055 697362

47 > Tre Pini

The small church of San Giuseppe Artigiano was the last work designed by Raffaello Fagnoni. Each material in this architecture is used to feature its natural expressive capacity. Exposed concrete for the left-hand wall, showing the traces of the wooden formwork; the bricks for the right-hand wall that curves around the apse, creating a poetic chiaroscuro effect; and the single sloping roof in reinforced brick with exposed internal surface. The baptismal font is placed near the entrance, protected by a curved concrete wall and lit by a round overhead skylight.
This bare, austere space is punctuated by a few simple elements: the rise towards the entrance, the passage through the baptismal font enclosure, the entry into the main nave where three steps lead to the raised altar level.
The solid external concrete wall is interrupted by a cross-frame window that protrudes in relation to the vertical surface enhanced with a multicoloured stained glass window designed by the architect. The bell-tower is composed of two vertical concrete sections with horizontal connecting slabs to reinforce the structure.

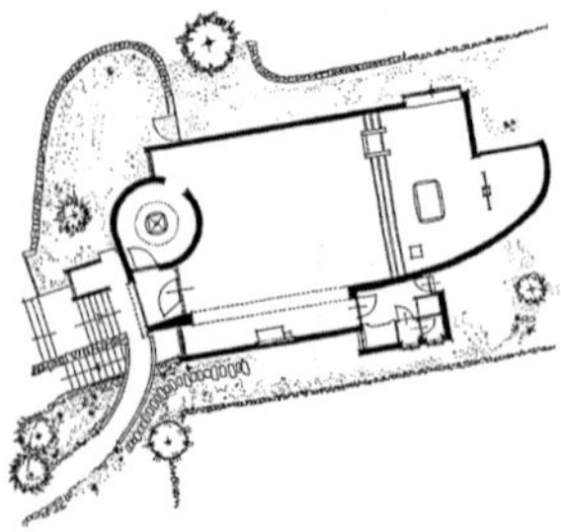

architects
Raffaello Fagnoni

type
church

construction
1965-1966

76. Rovezzano Quarter

Via di Rocca Tedalda
50136, Florence

external viewing only

14 > Rocca Tedalda

Rovezzano is on the eastern outskirts of Florence. It began in the early 1950s, when the mayor, Giorgio La Pira, launched a strong plan for the construction of social housing because of the post-war housing emergency. Following a competition launched by the city council, from 1951 to 1957, social housing designed by Domenico Cardini, Aurelio Cetica and Rodolfo Raspollini, was built in the area between the railway line, via della Ripa, the Mensola river, and Via di Rocca Tedalda. Apartment buildings were constructed with support structures in exposed brick and plaster-rendered hollow brick exteriors. In 1968, the district was extended with the addition of several tower blocks designed by Gianfranco Di Pietro and the Lega Studenti Architetti.
Later, in 1984 Gianfranco Di Pietro replaced some of the modest initial constructions, while maintaining the original town planning layout, constructing the buildings along an axis perpendicular to via Rocca Tedalda. This was composed of five parallel urban blocks, each comprised of two balconied buildings with common courtyards. The double buildings have gallery balconies that lead to small piazzas. The neighbourhood was also improved with the addition of public spaces, retail stores, and green parks to encourage interaction in the community.

architects
Gianfranco Di Pietro

type
residential

construction
1951-1957
1968
1984-1986

77. Sorgane Quarter

Viale Benedetto Croce,
Via Isonzo, Via Tagliamento
50126, Florence

external viewing only

23/48 > Croce

Following the successful intervention in Isolotto, and in answer to the urgent need for housing in the mid-1950s, the mayor, La Pira, launched a new social housing plan in the southern outskirts of Florence. This project was Sorgane, the first experiment in coordinated social housing (CEP).
The first project, designed by 7 groups of architects coordinated by Giovanni Michelucci, designed housing for 12,000 inhabitants in an urban system to be organised in two sections, in plains and on hillsides, integrating public spaces, residences and civic services. However, the plan was blocked because of a heated debate that led to the destruction of the local hillside area. This left only 4,000 apartments, designed by 3 groups coordinated by Ricci, Savioli and Poggi.
The urban layout is composed of a main north-south road, with perpendicular streets leading to apartment buildings and services. Although Poggi's style was quite conventional, Ricci and Savioli experimented with Brutalist architecture creating large-scale structures based on the Le Corbusier style. A well-planned street layout, designed to encourage communication among the inhabitants, and diverse structures built in exposed concrete and prefabricated elements, provided variety while giving the complex a coherent quality.

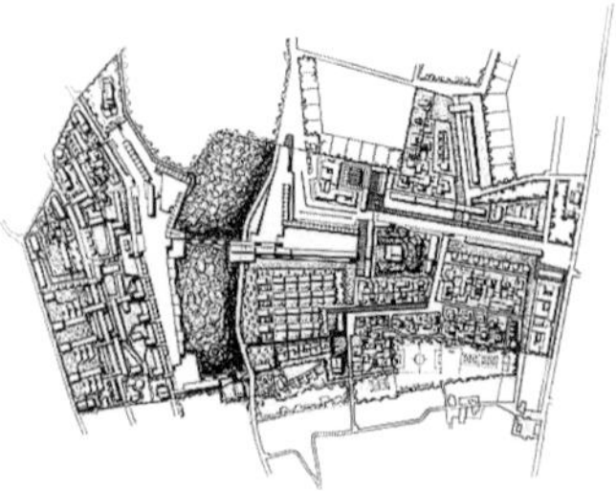

architects
Leonardo Ricci, Leonardo Savioli, Ferdinando Poggi

type
residential

construction
1954-1967

78. Giovanni da Verrazzano Bridge

Ponte Giovanni da Verrazzano
50126, Florence

open to the public

3/31/82 > De Sanctis

The Giovanni da Verrazzano bridge was built as the result of a competition launched by the Florence City Council, to redevelop the suburbs close to Florence by improving traffic flow and providing new pedestrian walkways. The project was designed by engineers, Carlo Damerini and Vittorio Scalesse and architect, Leonardo Savioli. This bridge differs from others because of the presence of a central steel girder composed of four Gerber beams, and a cantilever girder in prestressed, reinforced concrete at each end of the structure which absorb the load and transmit it to the foundations.
The bridge has a total length of 141 metres, maximum width of 26.80 metres and a maximum height of 12 metres; the single span measures 113 metres.
The designers developed a bridge that was not simply an infrastructure, but an integrated part of the city, communicating with the surrounding context: as well as the vehicle carriageways, the bridge slopes down at each side to the river level, to give pedestrians closer contact with the Arno. At each end of the bridge is a piazza that creates a contact with the neighbouring buildings and acts as a starting point for the pedestrian walkways which also incorporate panorama platforms for pausing to view the river.

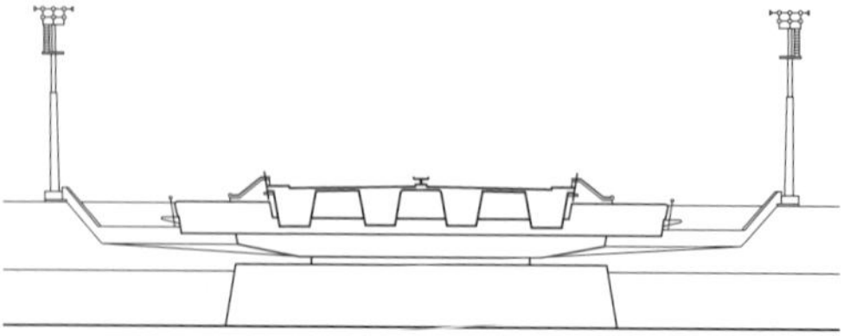

architects
Leonardo Savioli, Carlo Damerini, Vittorio Scalesse

type
bridge

construction
1967-1970

79. Emergency service 118 - Piero Palagi Hospital

Viale Michelangelo 41
50125, Florence

external viewing only

+39 055 6937249

www.asf.toscana.it

D > Istituto Ortopedico Toscano

This project involves an extension of the Piero Palagi Hospital, designed by Domenico Cardini and Rodolfo Raspollini, and built between 1965 and 1986. The complex is based on a comb structure that explains its unusual integration with the local terrain and landscape. It consists of a "backbone" extending down the hill slope, designed to link up five parallel blocks, orthogonal to the main axis; the blocks house medical wards and operating theatres.
The new General Care pavilion continues the same line as the existing buildings, completing the profile upstream, while interrupting the regular layout. The lower floor houses the Sterilisation and General Care departments, kitchen and laundry services, technical equipment rooms, and the upper floor, the Orthopaedics laboratory.
This is a construction with a limited footprint, built partially below ground, and with a low profile above ground. The architecture is inspired by traditional modest Tuscan construction. The stone paving of the access road recalls traditional materials, and is repeated on the first and part of the second level, and is used to face all the technical services area. Only the upper floor housing the Orthopaedics laboratory has a different façade: copper-finished steel strip cladding covers the walls, recalling the colours of the earth and the local landscape.

architects
Fabrizio Rossi Prodi

type
hospital

construction
2008-2014

80. Abbey of San Miniato al Monte

Via delle Porte Sante 34
50125, Florence

open to the public

+39 055 2342731
sanminiato@tin.it
www.sanminiatoalmonte.it

12 > San Miniato al Monte

Set on the hills above Florence, the Benedictine Abbey of San Miniato represents one of the finest examples of the Florentine Romanesque style which became a model for Renaissance architecture in later centuries. The first mention of a church dedicated to the martyr San Miniato, dates back to 783 AD. The Bishop Hildebrand wanted to rebuild the church completely in 1018, beginning construction work that continued throughout the whole 12th century. This was followed by the sacristy built in the 14th century, a chapel dedicated to the cardinal of Portugal, designed by Antonio Manetti, the bell tower by Baccio d'Agnolo, built in the 15th and 16th centuries, and the large external staircase constructed in the 19th century.
The gabled façade, completely faced in white Carrara and green Prato marble, is built on two levels: the lower band is composed of a row of five rounded blind arches to represent an entrance portico. On the upper portion, four Corinthian pilasters support a classical style tympanum. The long interior is composed of three naves, without a transept. It is built on three levels with a crypt, nave, and raised chancel, with a large rear apse decorated with mosaics. The internal marble facings are enhanced in the roof with painted wooden trusses, fine marble inlay work in the flooring, and frescoed walls.

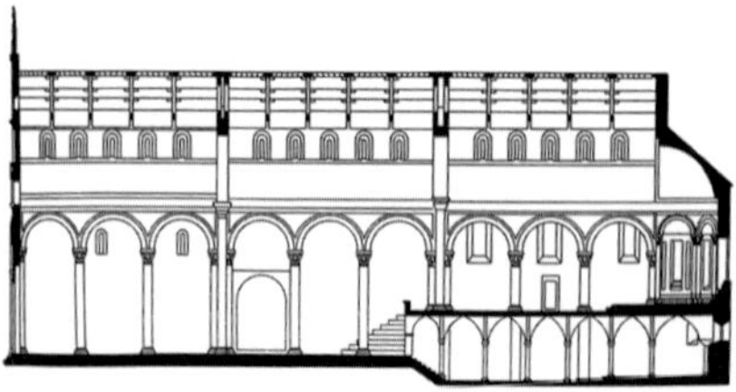

architects
Cardinal of Portugal Chapel:
Antonio Manetti
Bell tower: Baccio d'Agnolo

type
church, cemetery

construction
Church: 1018-uncertain date
Cardinal of Portugal Chapel:
1461-1466
Bell tower: 1524-1535

81. Villa Bayon

Via Beato Ippolito Galantini 10
50124, Florence

external viewing only

36/37 > San Gaggio

In 1963, Leonardo Savioli was commissioned by the Bayon family to design this villa as their residence on the San Gaggio hill, within a complex called Villaggio di San Francesco, designed by Savioli in the 1950s.
The architect did not follow the initial requests of the clients, and detached the architecture from references to the traditional Tuscan style, preferring to create a design independent of its context, in which the external shapes were inspired by a search for functional freedom and flexibility within the building.
The main idea behind the design was based on a structure positioned on supporting elements – high columns on the sides of the façade, and the large roof terrace in reinforced concrete. Below this is a sub-structure of two above-ground floors, composed of individual habitations, in which each space is designed as an independent element. On both the ground and upper floors, the living area is arranged as a single open flexible space, laid out on different levels, while the bedrooms are defined by sliding panels to create private zones.

architects
Leonardo Savioli

type
residential

construction
1965-1972

82. Misericordia Cemetery Extension

Via di Montisoni 14
50012, Bagno a Ripoli

January - March, October - December
Mon - Sat / 8.30 am - 5 pm
Sun / 8.30 am - 1 pm
April - September
Mon - Sat / 8.30 am - 6 pm
Sun / 8.30 am - 1 pm

+39 055 6233459
info@misericordia-antella.it
www.misericordia-antella.it

24/31 > Antella

The Misericordia cemetery, built in the mid-19th century, is a monumental cemetery with sculptures by famous artists such as Galileo Chini and Giuseppe Piombati Ammannati. Small extensions were made over the years until the final work was completed by Natalini Architetti.
The project included two new additions, a round courtyard, and an open courtyard linked with a portico, constructed to blend with the existing structure. While respecting the style of the existing cemetery, the new interventions are discernible for their simple clean and familiar style, including the choice of materials: white clinker tile or rendered walls, ceramic gres and stone paving, galvanised metal structures for the loggias, and porphyry blocks for external paving.
The portico links up the walkways of various levels, connecting the round courtyard, the existing buildings and the open courtyard. The round courtyard is surrounded by several trapezoidal chapels with openings in the rear walls to provide natural light and avoid a dark oppressive effect. The open courtyard has been built at the level of the first floor of the round courtyard and portico; a large planted lawn area slopes down, following the natural incline of the terrain.

© Natalini Architetti

architects
Natalini Architetti, Nazario Scelsi

type
cemetery

construction
1998-2008

83. Ugolino Golf Club

Via Chiantigiana per strada 3
50023, Impruneta

visiting on demand

+39 0552301009
info@golfugolino.it
www.golfugolino.it

365A/366A >
Poggio Ugolino

The Ugolino Golf complex sits on the slopes of the lower Chianti hills about 15 kilometers from the centre of Florence. Gherardo Bosio was commissioned to design the Club House in the very centre of the golf course terrain. Bosio's project also includes a swimming pool, diving board and platform in high-alumina cement with stainless steel stairs and hand-rail.

The building is a renowned and perfect example of Italian Rationalist Architecture. The design follows the horizontal lines of the surrounding landscape, and is composed of three blocks: the centre block is recessed in relation to the two side blocks. The entrance is composed of a wide glazed area on the ground floor of the centre block. Opposite the entrance, the staircase leads to the upper floors, while the ground floor houses services, offices and locker rooms. The first floor is composed of a large single space running along the length of the building, with generous windows that enclose the internal space and provide unrestricted views of the landscape. The top floor is divided into several smaller spaces for various activities.

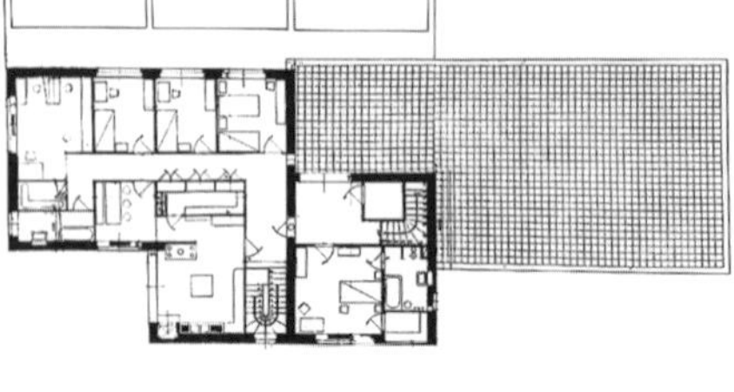

architects
Gherardo Bosio

type
club

construction
1934-1935

84. Autostrada del Sole Acoustic Barriers

Autostrada A1 -
Firenze-Bologna section
50023, Impruneta

open to the public

37 > I Bottai 01

The work to create a third lane on the Florence-Bologna motorway was not necessary only to improve the conditions of one of the busiest traffic stretches in the Italian road system and to provide far better flow to the city of Florence; it was also aimed at reducing noise levels and limiting the impact on the landscape as far as possible. The intervention by Archea Associati increased noise abatement for the communities living along the motorway, and also fulfilled all the conditions established by the Ministerial Decree, June 23, 1967, relative to landscape protection along motorways.
The intervention is located along a 10-km motorway section between Firenze Sud and Firenze Nord, but is not a solid wall. It is composed of a seemingly uniform single wall, but it allows travellers to see the landscape. It is a barrier but also a filter. These acoustic barriers are composed of micro perforated, Corten steel panels, supported by double-T beams, faced with long narrow strips of terracotta. The rock wool filled panels guarantee excellent noise abatement efficiency and the Impruneta terracotta is smog and frost-proof, thereby reducing maintenance costs considerably. This intervention blends harmoniously with the landscape through its materials, colour, and formal design.

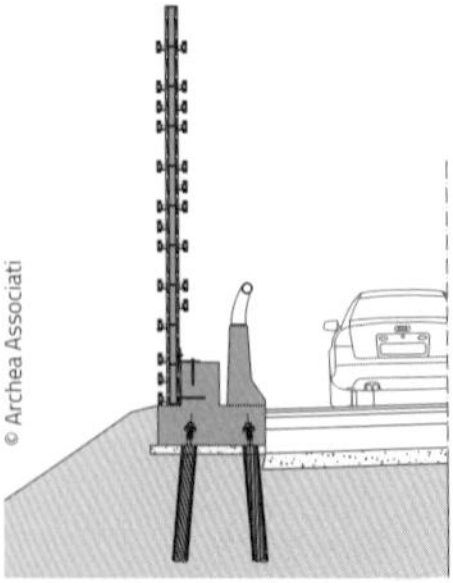

© Archea Associati

architects
Archea Associati

type
infrastructure

construction
2000-2007

Museums

Forte di Belvedere
Temporary contemporary art exhibitions
-
Via San Leonardo 1, 50125 Florence

museicivicifiorentini.comune.fi.it/fortebelvedere
info@muse.comune.fi.it
Tel +39 055 2616788

Galleria dell'Accademia
Medieval and Renaissance art
-
Via Ricasoli 58/60, 50122 Florence

www.galleriaaccademiafirenze.beniculturali.it
ga-afi@beniculturali.it
Tel +39 055 2388609

La Specola
Natural History museum
-
Via Romana 17, 50125 Florence

www.msn.unifi.it
edumsn@unifi.it
Tel +39 055 2756444

Museo Galileo
Medici and Lorenese scientific instrument collection
-
Piazza dei Giudici 1, 50122 Florence

www.museogalileo.it
info@museogalileo.it
Tel +39 055 265311

Museo degli Innocenti
Museum of the Istituto degli Innocenti Historic and Artistic Heritage
-
Piazza della Santissima Annunziata 13, 50122 Florence

www.istitutodeglinnocenti.it
info@istitutodeglinnocenti.it
Tel +39 055 20371

Museo Marino Marini
Modern art
-
Piazza di San Pancrazio, 50123 Florence

www.museomarinomarini.it
info@museomarinomarini.it
Tel +39 055 219432

Museo Nazionale del Bargello
Medieval and Renaissance Art
-
Via del Proconsolo 4, 50122 Florence

bargellomusei.beniculturali.it
mn-bar@beniculturali.it
Tel +39 055 2388606

Museo Novecento
Modern Art
-
Piazza Santa Maria Novella 10, 50123 Florence

www.museonovecento.it
comunicazione.cultura@comune.fi.it
Tel +39 055 286132

Museo dell'Opera del Duomo
Piazza del Duomo Religious Complex
Medieval and Renaissance art
-
Piazza del Duomo 9, 50122 Florence

www.ilgrandemuseodelduomo.it
opera@operaduomo.firenze.it
Tel +39 055 2302885

Museo Salvatore Ferragamo
Ferragamo Collection,
temporary exhibition
-
Piazza Santa Trinita 5/R, 50123 Florence

www.ferragamo.com
museoferragamo@ferragamo.com
Tel +39 055 3562846

Museo di San Marco
Renaissance Art
-
Piazza San Marco 3, 50121 Florence

www.polomusealetoscana.beniculturali.it
pm-tos.mussanmarco-fi@beniculturali.it
Tel +39 055 2388608

Palazzo Pitti
Palatina Gallery, Gallery of Modern Art, Royal Apartments, Fashion and Costume Gallery
-
Piazza de' Pitti 1, 50125 Florence

www.uffizi.it
ga-uff@beniculturali.it
Tel +39 055 23885

Palazzo Strozzi
Temporary art exhibitions
-
Piazza degli Strozzi, 50123 Florence

www.palazzostrozzi.org
info@palazzostrozzi.org
Tel +39 055 2645155

Uffizi
Medieval and Renaissance Art
-
Piazzale degli Uffizi 6, 50122 Florence

www.uffizi.it
ga-uff@beniculturali.it
Tel +39 055 23885

Theatres

Cinema Odeon
-
Piazza Strozzi, 50123 Florence

www.odeonfirenze.com
direzione@odeonfirenze.com
Tel +39 055 295051

Opera di Firenze
-
Piazzale Vittorio Gui 1, 50144 Florence

www.operadifirenze.it
sovrintendenza@maggiofiorentino.com
Tel +39 055 2779309

Cinema La Compagnia
-
Via Camillo Cavour 50/R, 50121 Florence

www.cinemalacompagnia.it
info@cinemalacompagnia.it
Tel +39 055 268451

Teatro Goldoni
-
Via Santa Maria 15, 50125 Florence

www.operadifirenze.it
sovrintendenza@maggiofiorentino.com
Tel +39 055 2779283

Teatro della Pergola
-
via della Pergola 12/32, 50121 Florence

www.teatrodellapergola.com
biglietteria@teatrodellapergola.com
Tel +39 055 22641

Teatro Puccini
-
Via delle Cascine 41, 50144 Florence

www.teatropuccini.it
info@teatropuccini.it
Tel +39 055 362067

Teatro Verdi
-
Via Ghibellina 99, 50122 Florence

www.teatroverdifirenze.it
info@teatroverdionline.it
Tel +39 055 212320

Restaurants

• • • expensive
• • mid-range
• inexpensive

Borgo Santo Pietro
• • •
Lungarno Benvenuto Cellini 69/R, 50125 Florence

www.borgointhecity.com/it
info@borgointhecity.com
Tel +39 055 5535677

Brac
•
Via dei Vagellai 18/R, 50122 Florence

www.libreriabrac.net
info@libreriabrac.net
Tel +39 055 0944877

Cestello Ristoclub
• • •
Piazza di Cestello, 50124 Florence

www.cestelloristoclub.com
info@cestelloristoclub.com
Tel +39 055 2645364

Cibreo
• • •
Via dei Macci 122r, 50122 Florence

www.cibreo.com
Tel +39 055 2441100

Enoteca Pinchiorri
• • •
Via Ghibellina 87, 50122 Florence

www.enotecapinchiorri.it
ristorante@enotecapinchiorri.com
Tel +39 055 242757

Fishing Lab Alle Murate
• •
Via del Proconsolo 16r, 50122 Florence

www.fishinglab.it
Tel +39 055 240618

Il Santo Bevitore
• •
Via di Santo Spirito 64/66 r, 50125 Florence

www.ilsantobevitore.com
info@ilsantobevitore.com
Tel +39 055 211264

Lungarno 23
•
Lungarno Torrigiani 23, 50125 Florence

www.lungarno23.it
info@lungarno23.it
Tel +39 055 2345957

Ménagère
••
Via de' Ginori 8/R, 50123 Florence

www.lamenagere.it
info@lamenagere.it
Tel +39 055 0750600

Ora D'Aria
•••
Via dei Georgofili 11R, 50122 Florence

www.oradariaristorante.com
info@oradariaristorante.com
Tel +39 055 2001699

Perseus
••
Viale Don Giovanni Minzoni 10/R, 50129 Florence

www.casatrattoria.com/ristorante-perseus-firenze
perseusfirenze@casatrattoria.com
Tel +39 055 588226

Trattoria 13 Gobbi
••
Via del Porcellana 9R, 50123 Florence

www.casatrattoria.com/trattoria-13-gobbi
info@casatrattoria.com
Tel +39 055 284015

Hotels

Benci House
•
Via dei Benci 15, 50122 Florence

www.bencihouse.it
info@bencihouse.com
Tel +39 393 8529081

••• expensive
•• mid-range
• inexpensive

Firenze Number Nine Wellness Hotel
••
Via Dei Conti 9, 50123 Florence

www.firenzenumbernine.com
Reception@firenzenumbernine.com
Tel +39 055 293777

Florence Old Bridge B&B
•
Via de' Guicciardini 22, 50125 Florence

www.florenceoldbridge.com
info@florenceoldbridge.com
Tel +39 055 2654262

Four Seasons Hotel
•••
Borgo Pinti 99, 50121 Florence

www.fourseasons.com/florence
Tel +39 055 26261

Gallery Art Hotel
•••
Vicolo dell'Oro 5, 50123 Florence

www.lungarnocollection.com
gallery@lungarnocollection.com
Tel +39 055 27263

Grand Hotel Minerva
• • •
Piazza di Santa Maria Novella 16,
50123 Florence

www.grandhotelminerva.com
info@grandhotelminerva.com
Tel +39 055 27230

NH Collection Firenze Porta Rossa
• •
Via Porta Rossa 19, 50123 Florence

www.nh-collection.com
nhcollectionportarossa@nh-hotels.com
Tel +39 055 2710911

Palazzo Alfieri Luxury Suites
•
Lungarno Corsini 2, 50123 Florence

www.palazzoalfieri.it
info@palazzoalfieri.it
Tel +39 055 2302185

Plaza Hotel Lucchesi
• •
Lungarno della Zecca Vecchia 38,
50122 Florence

www.hotelplazalucchesi.it
lucchesi@toflorence.it
Tel +39 055 26236

Plus Hostels Florence
•
Via Santa Caterina D'Alessandria 15,
50129 Florence

www.plushostels.com/it/plusflorence
info@plusflorence.com
Tel +39 055 6286347

The Westin Excelsior, Firenze
• • •
Piazza Ognissanti 3, 50123 Florence

www.westinflorence.com
excelsiorflorence@westin.com
Tel +39 055 27151

Architectural offices

Archea Associati
-
Lungarno Benvenuto Cellini 13, 50125
Florence

www.archea.it
staff@archea.it
Tel +39 055 6580127

ARX
-
Via degli Artisti 18/R, 50132 Florence

www.arxnet.net
studio@arxnet.net
Tel +39 055 9755168

Breschistudio associati
-
Via Enrico Mayer 16, 50134 Florence

www.breschistudio.com
breschistudio@me.com
Tel +39 055 363619

Claudio Nardi Architects
-
Via Ippolito Pindemonte 63, 50124
Florence

www.claudionardi.it
info@claudionardi.it
Tel +39 055 222132

CSPE
-
Piazzale Donatello 29, 50132 Florence

www.cspe.net
staff@cspe.net
Tel +39 055 5000701

DEFERRARI+MODESTI
-
Via Gino Capponi 23, 50121 Florence

www.deferrari-modesti.com
info@deferrari-modesti.com
Tel +39 055 5120335

Elio Di Franco
-
Via Sant'Egidio 15, 50122 Florence

Tel +39 055 2346292

Eutropia Architettura
-
Via Arnolfo 43, 50121 Florence

www.eutropia-architettura.it
info@eutropia-architettura.it
Tel +39 055 2466191

Fabio Capanni
-
Via del Romito 2, 50134 Florence

www.fabiocapanni.it
studio@fabiocapanni.it
Tel +39 055 484971

Ipostudio
-
Piazza Giuseppe Poggi 1, 50125 Florence

www.ipostudio.it
ipostudio@ipostudio.it
Tel +39 055 244041

Marco Dezzi Bardeschi
-
Viale Filippo Strozzi 24, 50129 Florence

www.marcodezzibardeschi.com
madezzib@tin.it
Tel +39 055 474872

Natalini Architetti
-
Via del Salviatino 10/A, 50137 Florence

www.nataliniarchitetti.com
natalini.architetti@tin.it
Tel +39 055 600400

Progettisti Associati Annalisa Baracchi e Giuliano Galzigni
-
Viale Antonio Gramsci 24, 50132 Florence

Tel +39 055 2466366

Rossiprodi Associati
-
Via Guglielmo Marconi 29, 50131 Florence

www.rossiprodi.it
info@rossiprodi.it
Tel +39 055 583759

Studio di Architettura Galli e Gueli
-
Viale Antonio Gramsci 18, 50132 Florence

www.galliegueli.it
info@galliegueli.it
Tel +39 055 241042

Studio Macci & Partners
-
Via Paolo Boselli 2, 50136 Florence

www.studiomacciarchitetti.com
studioabaco@tin.it
Tel +39 055 690847

studiostudio architettiurbanisti
-
Via Pisana 175, 50143 Florence

www.studiostudio.it
mail@studiostudio.it

Index by architect

Index by project

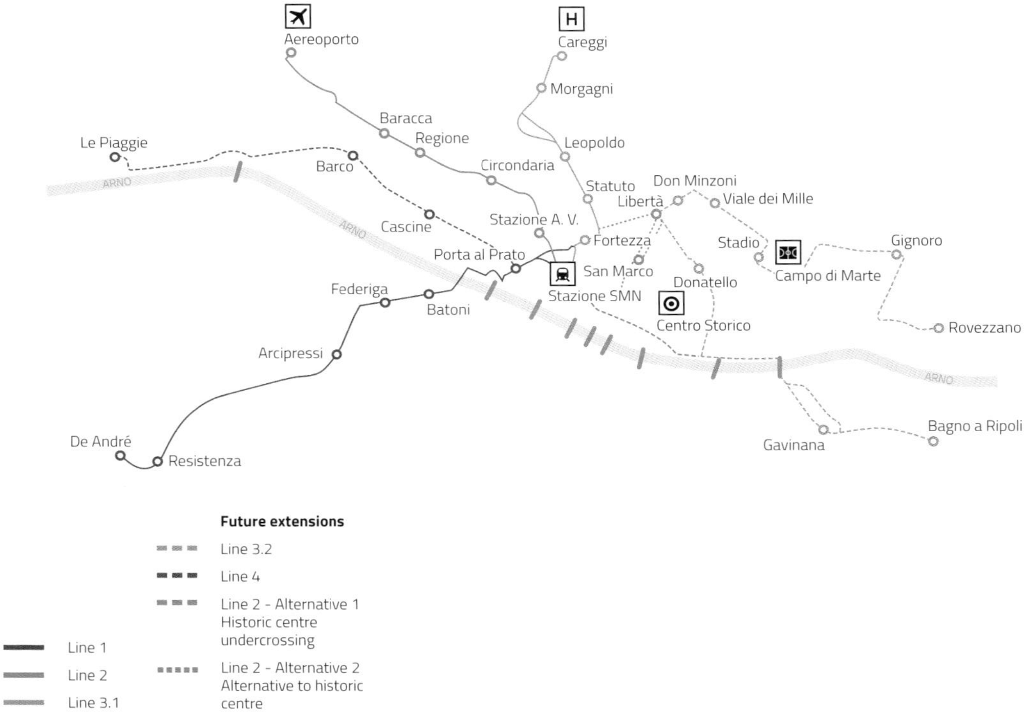
Aereoporto
Careggi
Morgagni
Baracca
Regione
Le Piaggie
Barco
Leopoldo
Circondaria
ARNO
Statuto
Don Minzoni
Libertà
Viale dei Mille
Cascine
Stazione A. V.
Fortezza
Stadio
Gignoro
Porta al Prato
San Marco
Campo di Marte
Federiga
Donatello
Batoni
Stazione SMN
Centro Storico
Rovezzano
Arcipressi
ARNO
Bagno a Ripoli
De André
Resistenza
Gavinana
Future extensions
Line 3.2
Line 4
Line 2 - Alternative 1 Historic centre undercrossing
Line 1
Line 2
Line 3.1
Line 2 - Alternative 2 Alternative to historic centre

Fortezza da basso
Piazza Indipendenza
Stazione S. Maria Novella
ataf point
Piazza Unità
San Lorenzo
Piazza S. Marco
Piazza S.S. Annunziata
Ospedale S. Maria Nuova
Piazza S. Maria Novella
Piazza del Duomo
Piazza della Signoria
Piazza S.S. Firenze
Piazza del Carmine
Ponte Vecchio
Piazza S. Spirito
Ponte alle Grazie